Beginnings

and Endings

[and what happens in between]

Beginnings

and Endings

[and what happens in between]

Maggi Dawn

Daily Bible readings from Advent to Epiphany

Text copyright © Maggi Dawn 2007
The author asserts the moral right
to be identified as the author of this work

Published by
The Bible Reading Fellowship
First Floor, Elsfield Hall
15–17 Elsfield Way, Oxford OX2 8FG
Website: www.brf.org.uk

ISBN 978 1 84101 566 8
First published 2007
10 9 8 7 6 5 4 3 2 1 0
All rights reserved

Acknowledgments
Unless otherwise stated, scripture quotations are taken from The New Revised Standard Version of the Bible, Anglicized Edition, copyright © 1989, 1995 by the Division of Christian Education of the National Council of the Churches of Christ in the USA, and are used by permission. All rights reserved.

Scripture taken from the New American Standard Bible, copyright © 1960, 1962, 1963, 1968, 1971, 1972, 1973, 1975, 1977, 1995 by The Lockman Foundation. Used by permission.

Extracts from the Authorized Version of the Bible (The King James Bible), the rights in which are vested in the Crown, are reproduced by permission of the Crown's patentee, Cambridge University Press.

A catalogue record for this book is available from the British Library

Printed in Singapore by Craft Print International Ltd

Contents

Introduction 7

Section 1: Where do I begin? The Gospels and the salvation story

1 Dec Early or late? 12
2 Dec John: let's start at the very beginning 17
3 Dec Luke: let me tell you a story 21
4 Dec Luke: flashback 24
5 Dec Matthew: what's in a name? 28
6 Dec Mark: where the action is 31
7 Dec Adam and Eve: the end of the beginning 34

Section 2: In between: patriarchs and promises

8 Dec Abraham's call 40
9 Dec Land and promise 44
10 Dec Redigging the wells 47

Section 3: Prophets and heralds

11 Dec Calling down fire: who's setting the agenda? 54
12 Dec Eat, drink, sleep 59
13 Dec Not in the fire... 63
14 Dec The beginning of the end 67
15 Dec Every valley shall be exalted 71
16 Dec Gaudete Sunday: already and not yet 75

Section 4: Angels and announcements: how does God speak to us, and how do we hear?

17 Dec Unclean lips and the problem of language 80
18 Dec Zechariah: the man who had waited too long 85

19 Dec Don't hurry: perplexed and pondering 90
20 Dec Questioning God 94
21 Dec On the margins..96

Section 5: The Holy Family: the timeless in the everyday

22 Dec Coming, ready or not 102
23 Dec From now on... 106
24 Dec Magnificat: a promise and a call 110
25 Dec No room at the inn? 114
26 Dec Dirty or clean 118
27 Dec The Word became flesh...120
28 Dec Joseph...124
29 Dec Fear, worship and wide-eyed wonder....................127
30 Dec The man who is God 132

Section 6: Endings (and new beginnings)

31 Dec The end is where we started (endings and Mark)..138
1 Jan Waiting and longing 143
2 Jan Shepherds and wise men.......................................147
3 Jan Double-edged prophecy 151
4 Jan Born in a borrowed room 155
5 Jan Kings and gifts 159
6 Jan The end is a new beginning: returning by another way 164

Introduction

Advent marks the beginning of the Church year and a time of preparation for the celebration of the coming of Christ into the world. It marks the beginning of the Christian era in the birth of Christ, and it looks further back to ancient roots in the lives of the patriarchs, in the earliest human stories of Adam and Eve, and into the timeless eternity of our beginnings in God. So there is an obvious connection between Advent and beginnings.

Advent is also about endings, though, because it anticipates the second coming of Christ. In Christian belief, this idea symbolizes the end of the present era and the fulfilment of the kingdom of God. It's a clearly held hope within the Christian faith, yet at the same time, like all future hopes, it is shrouded in mystery because precisely what the hope means in reality is as yet hidden from us. Here, too, the Bible tantalizes us with promises that cannot be fully understood.

The biblical accounts of beginnings and endings are incomplete, and don't give us the crystal clarity of factual evidence that we would sometimes like the Bible to deliver. But this does not indicate that they have no meaning for us. Even science and rational thought, in which we invest so much trust, cannot give us a full account of our beginnings, and the prediction of the end is even more a matter of conjecture and likelihood. The Bible is neither a scientific manual nor a magical book of fortune-telling. It does not aim to explain science or to predict the future; rather, it gives us stories, histories, songs, experience and spiritual meditations to aid us as we make sense of the lives we live and the world we inhabit.

The biblical accounts of beginnings and endings tell us that the Christian faith is a journey that starts somewhere and goes somewhere. It's a journey that develops through time, rather than simply going round and round in an endlessly repeating cycle. The season of Advent, too, reminds us that we come from somewhere and we are going somewhere, and thinking about beginnings and endings helps us to rediscover meaning and purpose as we live in these times that are 'in between'.

There have been periods in history when the Christian hope of a second coming and an afterlife has been used to mollify people instead of addressing issues of justice, or even to frighten Christians into submission. It is healthier to understand our faith as an anchor to the present and a way of discovering the possibility of living in freedom and enjoying depth and abundance in our life now. We do not live in the past, and neither do we want to hasten our own end.

The opening section of this book deals with 'beginnings', looking at how the Gospel writers and the writers of the Genesis accounts reveal their ideas about where our story begins. The following sections touch on each of the themes symbolized by the candles in an Advent wreath—the patriarchs, the prophets, John the Baptist and Mary, the mother of Jesus. Each of these themes marks a stage, a new beginning, in the story of salvation, and each of them looks toward the ending in a fresh way.

In between, we shall pause to consider 'angels and announcements'. The nativity stories are renowned for the appearance of angels announcing new beginnings. This section connects them up with some older stories about angels and offers some meditations on how we hear God's voice and how we respond to the call to new beginnings in our own lives.

The holy family themselves become the focus of our readings in the first week of Christmas. As we look back on their story, we see how it dramatically marks the end of one era and the beginning of another. Yet, as they themselves lived through it, it was as much a time in-between as our lives are now. This family has much to teach us about the meeting of heaven and earth, the extraordinary and the ordinary, within everyday life.

Finally we will look at endings in the Bible, although (and I hope this isn't too much of a spoiler!) we shall discover that as the Christian faith is built on the hope of resurrection, endings are always new beginnings.

I invite you to join me in this meditation on *Beginnings and Endings* this Advent. It has been a real pleasure to write on a theme that seems to open up new depths every year, and I hope that you will enjoy these meditations as much as I have enjoyed writing them. I wish you a happy Advent.

[SECTION 1]

Where do I begin? The Gospels and the salvation story

The beginning of Advent is a beginning in a number of different ways. Advent is an ancient season of preparation, both for the celebration of the first coming of Christ into the world and for the anticipation of his second coming. There are themes that carry us through Advent, which are highlighted by traditional readings and by an Advent wreath with four or five symbolic candles.

The first Sunday of Advent is the beginning of the Church year, the liturgical journey that explores not only the story but the meaning of salvation. Creation as the start of everything is a theme that is often highlighted at this time.

It is also the beginning of our preparations for Christmas—and, as Christmas celebrations are creeping further and further back into December, Advent is focused more on Christmas than it ever used to be. The preparation for Christmas, and the stories of the nativity, are a key part of the later weeks of Advent.

This first section of the book will visit these overlapping ideas and will also include a look at the beginning of each of the four Gospels, to see how their chosen starting places for the story of salvation connect up to the big themes of Advent.

[1 December]

Early or late?

The Lord is my light and my salvation; whom shall I fear?
The Lord is the stronghold of my life; of whom shall I be afraid?
When evildoers assail me to devour my flesh—
my adversaries and foes—they shall stumble and fall.
Though an army encamp against me, my heart shall not fear;
though war rise up against me, yet I will be confident.
One thing I asked of the Lord, that will I seek after:
to live in the house of the Lord all the days of my life,
to behold the beauty of the Lord, and to inquire in his temple.
For he will hide me in his shelter in the day of trouble;
he will conceal me under the cover of his tent;
he will set me high on a rock.
Now my head is lifted up above my enemies all around me,
and I will offer in his tent sacrifices with shouts of joy;
I will sing and make melody to the Lord.
Hear, O Lord, when I cry aloud, be gracious to me and answer me!
'Come,' my heart says, 'seek his face!'
Your face, Lord, do I seek. Do not hide your face from me.
Do not turn your servant away in anger, you who have been my help.
Do not cast me off, do not forsake me, O God of my salvation!
If my father and mother forsake me, the Lord will take me up.
Teach me your way, O Lord,
and lead me on a level path because of my enemies.
Do not give me up to the will of my adversaries,
for false witnesses have risen against me,
and they are breathing out violence.
I believe that I shall see the goodness of the Lord
in the land of the living.

Wait for the Lord;
be strong, and let your heart take courage;
wait for the Lord!

PSALM 27

If you're reading this on the first of December, you may well already have had a Christmas card or two fall through your letter box. I love receiving Christmas cards, from the first ones that arrive on the first of December and those that arrive with a slightly panicked message of lateness on Christmas Eve, to those that come with a sheepish apology around the third of January. Whenever they arrive, early or late, I'm always cheered up by this annual reminder of how many good friends I have.

I have to admit that I find it slightly depressing that Christmas always seems to begin way ahead of schedule, when shop displays and Christmas lights go up in November or even earlier. So when the very first cards arrive in the first few days of December, I'm usually still feeling a bit 'bah-humbuggy' about it all! But when the last posting day is upon us and I realize I'm behind schedule, then I envy the foresight of my early-bird friends and vow to be more like them next year. Certainly Christmas can sometimes feel less like a feast to be celebrated and more like a deadline to be reached. It's often, though not always, the woman in a household who carries the stress of having everything ready for Christmas, but Christmas creates deadlines for all sorts of other people too—church leaders, school teachers, retailers and many others. Such moments focus very sharply our sense of time, and of being bound by time.

In devotional terms, though, following the seasons of the Church year can leave us with this feeling that things never happen at the right time. The realities of life rarely match up with the mood of the Church year: they always come too early or too late. If, as we travel through Lent or Advent, life is delivering abundant joys and happiness, the sombre tone of the season never quite hits home. But it's even harder to deal with if you are feeling down or low when Christmas or Easter arrives. A few years ago, a friend and I wrote to each other all the way through Lent, sharing our reflections on the season. She was a great devotee of retreats and silent space; I was the mother of a newborn baby, and silent spaces were few and far between. Our Lenten experience was quite profound that year, as we were both going through extreme lows for quite different reasons. On Easter Day my friend emailed to say, 'I'm so fed up with the Church year. Resurrection? I don't think so. I feel like I need to stay in Good Friday for a good long time yet.'

All too often we have this dislocated feeling of being out of time, out of step, and Christmas is a particularly difficult season to negotiate if you don't feel like celebrating. It's not only the Church but the whole culture that feeds us an exaggerated image of happiness and celebration, which sets us up to feel very low if we are not in a party mood. Most of our life is lived in this in-between place where things come early or late, but never on time.

Psalm 27 is sometimes given the title 'A triumphant song of confidence'. I think it reads more like a defiant song than a triumphant one. The way the psalmist mixes up his tenses creates an interesting effect of reflecting on past promises fulfilled, asking for something to happen right now, stating that it's already happened and confidently predicting that it will happen in the future. He seems, at one and the same time, to be giving thanks for something that is already here and asking for help in the midst of trouble. There's an urgent anxiety about his cry for help: 'Do not cast me off, do not forsake me...' (v. 9). Perhaps there's even a touch of the childish promise to be good if God will only help him: 'Teach me your way, O Lord, and lead me on a level path' (v. 11). The psalmist's experience reminds me of the dislocation of our lives from the Church seasons. God's gifts do not always come according to our timetable or at the moment when we think we need them. Advent and Christmas promise us God's presence, and yet it seems that sometimes God hides his face and is nowhere to be found. God's timetable is not the same as ours, and our sense of need or urgency doesn't twist God's arm into a response.

When I was a child, we had a maiden aunt, a remarkable and

wonderful woman, who always, absolutely dependably, forgot all our birthdays. But at some random time of year—May or July or November—a big parcel would arrive full of presents. They might say 'Happy Birthday' or 'Happy Christmas', regardless of the time of year. It seemed madly exciting to us to get a completely unexpected present just when life was going through a tedious moment. It was always books (she taught English literature, and was bang up to date on the latest releases) and they were always wonderful. The same aunt, when we went to stay, would sneak into our bedroom just before sunrise, pull jumpers over our pyjamas, and put our bare feet into shoes with *no socks* (against Mum's rules!), and quietly exit the house with us, leaving everyone else asleep. Then she would pile my sister and me into her very old Austin and drive us down to the beach. This was in Somerset, where the beach goes out for about two miles at low tide. There she would actually drive across the sand—again, strictly against the rules, but there's no one there at sunrise to make you obey the rules—and out of the car would appear a Primus stove, an omelette pan, eggs, butter, salt, pepper and fresh bread. We ate omelettes and drank tea as the sun rose over the sea, and then went paddling in our pyjamas, breathing in great gulps of early morning salty air. The woman was a genius, and we adored her.

Whenever I forget a Christmas card, a birthday card or whatever, I think of Auntie Margaret. Please, God, let me be like her. I hope I never become the kind of person who demands diamonds and perfume on the right date. I hope I do become the kind of person who remembers to send gifts that someone will love, instead of gifts to satisfy a deadline. Whenever God's gifts elude me—when there is no joy at Easter, no wonder at Christmas, or simply no sense of God's presence in between times—again I think of Auntie Margaret. The gift will arrive at the right moment, even if not on the 'right' date. Joy on demand is joyless indeed, but omelettes on the beach and presents in July, I can seriously live with.

If we confidently depend on the knowledge that God's gifts, unlike Santa's, are not delivered to a deadline, then we can live within the seasons knowing that the gift they represent will come to us, unexpectedly, not necessarily on time. We can say with hope, or even a little holy defiance, 'I believe that I shall see the goodness of the Lord in the land of the living' (v. 13).

[2 December]

John: let's start at the very beginning

In the beginning when God created the heavens and the earth, the earth was a formless void and darkness covered the face of the deep, while a wind from God swept over the face of the waters. Then God said, 'Let there be light'; and there was light. And God saw that the light was good; and God separated the light from the darkness. God called the light Day, and the darkness he called Night. And there was evening and there was morning, the first day.

GENESIS 1:1–5

In the beginning was the Word, and the Word was with God, and the Word was God. He was in the beginning with God. All things came into being through him, and without him not one thing came into being. What has come into being in him was life, and the life was the light of all people. The light shines in the darkness, and the darkness did not overcome it.

JOHN 1:1–5

Where does a story begin? A storyteller can always start from any one of a number of different points, and choosing the starting point is an important decision, because the way a story begins dramatically affects the way the reader understands and interprets it. The beginning needs to be intriguing enough to make us want to read on, it has to give the initial threads that draw the reader into the plot, and it sets up clues as to how to interpret all the information that follows.

Where would you begin if you were telling the story of salvation?

You might decide to start where the 'action' of the story begins, with the life and ministry of Jesus, his teaching and miracles and conversations with disciples and friends. Of course, Jesus didn't just come from nowhere, so you might start the story with his birth and add a bit of his childhood and some family history. There again, it would give a bit of context if you told something of the history of Jesus' people, and how they were expecting a Messiah—so perhaps you'd start with the prophets, or even all the way back at Abraham. Come to that, you could go right back to the story of Adam and Eve: that would give you a way of showing why the human race needs salvation in the first place. Where you choose to begin the story affects the way the rest of it is understood. Matthew, Mark, Luke and John begin their Gospels very differently, and through their choice of starting place each one gives the story a different slant, a different angle on Jesus, a different focus of theological truth.

A lot of the time when we read the Gospels, we try to make a complete story out of four different accounts, filling in the gaps in one with material from the others. But to achieve this completeness, we sacrifice something of the vitality of each individual account. It's worth separating them out, and noticing their differences, as if we were focusing on different facets of a diamond.

Perhaps the most famous and distinctive opening of all is that of the Gospel of John, so often heard read at carol services, or on Christmas Eve or Christmas Day. And the most obvious thing about it is how closely it echoes the opening words of Genesis. Why did John borrow these ancient words to start his Gospel?

I think this borrowing trick does two interesting things. The first is to show that from John's point of view, the beginning of the salvation story is set firmly at the beginning of everything. John doesn't think of this beginning as a point in time, though, but in a conceptual, philosophical sense. He is painting a picture of a pre-human Christ—long before the birth of Jesus of Nazareth—who is part of the God who is the source of all meaning, all life and all being. So John begins the salvation story in the arena of mystical philosophy.

Some readers of John's Gospel think that he was too mystical in his approach to Jesus: they find his picture of Jesus undeniably divine but not quite convincingly human. He may indeed lean quite far on the side of mysticism, but he is, I think, trying to draw attention to the way that Jesus embodies a paradoxical meeting of the mystical and the material—or, if you like, connects heaven and earth. 'The Word was with God, and the Word was God,' he tells us (v. 1), leaving us in no doubt about Jesus' divinity—but now he is here in time and space. For John, the salvation story begins right back in the unknowable mysteries of eternity, but he goes on to tell us that Jesus was the means of breaking through the inaccessibility of that mystical beyond: 'The Word became flesh and lived among us' (1:14).

When someone borrows a quotation and makes a new literary classic from it, it affects the original work as well as the new one. By borrowing the opening words of Genesis, John not only grabs hold of an old and well-known phrase to launch his own story, he also gives a new twist to the way the original words are read. Once you've read the words 'In the beginning…' in John's poetic-philosophical rendition, you realize that Genesis itself is open to the same philosophical reading—that this beginning too is not only a chronological beginning but a way of exploring the idea that the source and the purpose of our life reside in God. The human search for beginnings is much bigger than a desire for factual information, and a religious account is not a soft option for those who can't cope with science. It's a different kind of search altogether.

It's not exactly true to say that Genesis is *un*historical. Writings from other ancient communities in the Mediterranean basin also contain accounts that follow the same big themes as the Genesis stories, of a creation, a garden and later a warning of a flood and a family that survived in a boat. It seems likely that these ancient accounts emerge from the collective memory of prehistorical events, and geological and archeological finds endorse this view. As archeologist C. Leonard Woolley wrote in 1934, 'We need not try to make history out of legend, but we ought to assume that beneath much that is artificial or incredible there lurks something of fact.'[1]

The stories in Genesis 1—11 may contain something of what we understand as history, but they are also 'mythical'—not in the sense that they are like fairy tales with no serious consequence, but in the sense that they are trying to do more than just deliver factual information. They are exploring truths about human life and existence that can't be assessed by popping them in a test tube or through a computer program. To get the full picture of human life and meaning, we need more than science alone: we need poetry and philosophy, story and history, art and music. Songs, poems and novels are all forms of writing that don't necessarily claim to be factually true, yet they have a capacity to communicate something about life that is true in a different and perhaps deeper sense. The stories in the opening chapters of Genesis are *teleological*—told to demonstrate that the meaning and purpose of human life are rooted in God, rather than to give a scientific or chronological account of our origins. In that sense, Genesis is bang up to date. It's doing what human beings have always done: making sense of why we're here, why we're the way we are, and where we're going.

It's useful to remember, especially when popular media coverage gives the impression that science and religion are in opposition to each other, that treating Genesis as myth, philosophy or story is nothing new. To read it this way is not a thin, 21st-century apology for a religion that can't defend itself against the march of science, but a different way of thinking altogether. John shows us that, as far back as the first or second century, Christian writers have long been able to distinguish between the mystical and the rational, and between poetry and factual reportage.

John, then, borrows the poetic beginning of Genesis, using it to show that the story of Jesus began right back at the beginning of everything. In so doing, he shifts the ground for the interpretation of Genesis, showing us that the scriptures have always had the poetic capacity for reinterpretation, not to change their meaning beyond recognition but to carry the threads of its meaning from one age to the next.

[3 December]

Luke: let me tell you a story

Since many have undertaken to set down an orderly account of the events that have been fulfilled among us, just as they were handed on to us by those who from the beginning were eyewitnesses and servants of the word, I too decided, after investigating everything carefully from the very first, to write an orderly account for you, most excellent Theophilus, so that you may know the truth concerning the things about which you have been instructed.

In the days of King Herod of Judea, there was a priest named Zechariah, who belonged to the priestly order of Abijah. His wife was a descendant of Aaron, and her name was Elizabeth. Both of them were righteous before God, living blamelessly according to all the commandments and regulations of the Lord. But they had no children, because Elizabeth was barren, and both were getting on in years.

LUKE 1:1–7

Luke's is the only one of the four Gospels to have this kind of prologue, a little introductory statement as to why and how the Gospel was written. It's a matter of long debate whether Theophilus was the name of a real person or whether the name, which means 'lover of God', was Luke's way of addressing his readers personally. Either way, the opening sentence has the effect of giving some sense of relationship between the storyteller and the reader. You get the sense that Luke is writing to you personally, not just addressing some nameless, faceless crowd.

Writing to real readers is one thing that makes Luke one of the best storytellers in the Bible. Another is the fact that he makes the people inside the story seem real too. Luke gives us more than historical plot, more than philosophy and doctrine: he gives us flesh-and-blood characters with whom we can identify. In particular, he is the only one of the Gospel writers who brings Jesus' family to life. Matthew tells us about the surrounding circumstances of the birth stories, but only Luke has the 'inside' information. He said in his prologue that he had carefully investigated everything 'from the very first' (v. 3)—meaning the start of Jesus life, perhaps? It's possible that Luke may have known members of the holy family, and perhaps he even knew Mary, the mother of Jesus, in person. He certainly had a source close to the family to get hold of these personal anecdotes.

Luke is a storyteller, but one with a respect for historical sense—he says he wants it to be an 'orderly' account (v. 1)—and his reason for telling the story is that he wants to pass on the faith. The words he uses in the prologue are the words of a teacher: he speaks of what has been 'handed on' (v. 2), taught from one group to the next, and he speaks of the story as both 'truth' and 'instruction' (v. 4). Luke, then, wants to give a rational and sensible account of the events that the Christian faith are based on, and he wants to tell it in such a way that it demands personal engagement with Jesus, not just rational assent to a belief system or obedience to religious ritual.

Luke's Gospel, more than any other, tells the story of Jesus in the most humanly engaged way. Luke's characters climb off the pages and touch our heartstrings, not just our intellect. It's Luke who gave us the great emotive and personal stories of the Gospels: the parental agony and sibling rivalry in the story of the prodigal son; the unexpected friendship of Jesus towards Zacchaeus; the weaving together of twelve years in the life of a woman and a girl, both of whom need new life; the confusion and pain of the disciples on the road to Emmaus. He declares his intent, in the opening verses of his Gospel, to give an account in the right order. The account he gives places events in time and focuses the story on the impact of Jesus upon real people.

Luke's starting place is a focus on human interest, not on history or prophecy, but he deftly gives the story context and definition by highlighting the fact that it takes place in the context of history, politics and religion. 'In the days of King Herod of Judea, there was a priest,' he begins (v. 5), and immediately tells us that the story begins in the temple in Jerusalem, the heart of first-century Judaism. It's a story about religious things but, as we shall see, a story that turns religious matters on their head. It's also a story that takes place in a political setting, in a nation under occupation, under the reign of a puppet king. That's important because the Gospel, as Luke tells it, has political consequences as well as religious ones. Then, he makes the story intensely personal by telling us that the priest and his wife 'were living blamelessly… but they had no children' (v. 6). In Zechariah and Elizabeth's cultural context, to be childless was not only a personal grief but also an implied slight on their character, as childlessness carried with it a sense of divine judgment.

Luke begins, then, by telling us that the good news of Jesus happens at a particular moment in history to real people. He sets the scene for what will be disrupted and challenged and brought to account by the gospel, and for what will be rescued and salvaged and healed. He sets the good news of Jesus not merely in a religious setting, but in the wider scheme of things. It's 'in the days of King Herod of Judea'—right in the midst of everyday life and political history—and Luke doesn't shy away from the fact that the gospel arrives in a time of injustice, in an area of war zones and occupied territories, disrupting existing political and religious hierarchies. The good news is full of life and goodness but it isn't well-behaved or polite. It is genuinely good news for real people—people who are faithful and good but also people who are broken-hearted, whose hopes have been dashed, who live under a shadow because society unjustly hangs a question mark over their heads. Luke begins the good news right in the heart of life: it will affect everything, political, religious, community and family. The gospel, for Luke, is not primarily conceptual. It's right here, right now, and it's thoroughly personal.

[4 December]

Luke: flashback

Now when all the people were baptized, and when Jesus also had been baptized and was praying, the heaven was opened, and the Holy Spirit descended upon him in bodily form like a dove. And a voice came from heaven, 'You are my Son, the Beloved; with you I am well pleased.'

Jesus was about thirty years old when he began his work. He was the son (as was thought) of Joseph son of Heli, son of Matthat, son of Levi, son of Melchi, son of Jannai, son of Joseph, son of Mattathias, son of Amos, son of Nahum, son of Esli, son of Naggai, son of Maath, son of Mattathias, son of Semein, son of Josech, son of Joda, son of Joanan, son of Rhesa, son of Zerubbabel, son of Shealtiel, son of Neri, son of Melchi, son of Addi, son of Cosam, son of Elmadam, son of Er, son of Joshua, son of Eliezer, son of Jorim, son of Matthat, son of Levi, son of Simeon, son of Judah, son of Joseph, son of Jonam, son of Eliakim, son of Melea, son of Menna, son of Mattatha, son of Nathan, son of David, son of Jesse, son of Obed, son of Boaz, son of Sala, son of Nahshon, son of Amminadab, son of Admin, son of Arni, son of Hezron, son of Perez, son of Judah, son of Jacob, son of Isaac, son of Abraham, son of Terah, son of Nahor, son of Serug, son of Reu, son of Peleg, son of Eber, son of Shelah, son of Cainan, son of Arphaxad, son of Shem, son of Noah, son of Lamech, son of Methuselah, son of Enoch, son of Jared, son of Mahalaleel, son of Cainan, son of Enos, son of Seth, son of Adam, son of God.

LUKE 3:21–38

I can almost hear you wondering... 'Surely this is a misprint? Isn't this one of those bits of the Bible that you skip over when you're reading it? Surely Maggi didn't mean to include that bit?' Or maybe, less charitably, you're wondering whether I've been living in a university for too long and have begun to lose touch with reality altogether... Well, stick with me here! This long list of names may seem like an odd little detour for Luke to make, just as he has got the story going, but it tells us something vitally important about where he thinks the story begins, and has serious theological implications for everything else that follows.

Of course it's obvious that this isn't 'the beginning' of Luke's Gospel, in the sense that it isn't the first chapter, but this list of names shows us where Luke traces back the beginning of the story chronologically. He has used an interesting literary structure here. We saw yesterday that he does his theology largely through the mode of storytelling, not apologetics or philosophy or journalistic reportage. Luke is the most accomplished narrator of stories, the most literary of the Gospel writers. He spends the first two chapters of his Gospel painting a vivid picture of two couples, in two generations of the same family. Elizabeth and Zechariah are a childless couple, already into middle age and beyond the hope of having children. Joseph and Mary are a young couple who are only just betrothed, so for Mary the expectation of a family is threatened (as her marriage might be called off) and, at the same time, brought forward with suddenness. There is a big element of surprise that these two couples, at opposite ends of their lives, are now expecting babies.

Once the stories of the births are over, there is a little vignette of Jesus' childhood, and then Luke flashes forward about 18 years, to the passage we have read today. He picks up the story of the two boys as adults, when Jesus comes to John to be baptized, and this brings us to the brink of the real story—the point where the action is going to start. Then, just as Jesus has entered the frame, this list of the whole family history is inserted as another flashback sequence. It's a bit like one of those movies that starts with a bit of storyline and then cuts to a completely different scene with the caption 'London, ten years earlier'—except that in this case the flashback sequence moves right back through the whole family tree. You can imagine the dreamlike effect if this were actually a movie, every frame showing another man with his family, each looking strikingly similar to the last one, but with the clothes and scenery becoming more and more archaic as the time frame moves backwards.

Using this flashback and flashforward technique, Luke has got us to the beginning of the story of Jesus' ministry via a patchwork of images, each of which has shown us something of what led up to this moment, what made Jesus significant, why the camera is now trained on him and not on someone else.

Via this historical flashback, Luke indicates that the chronological beginning of the story goes right back to Adam, at the beginning of the human race. John, as we saw earlier, places the beginning of the story before time began, to ground the idea of Jesus philosophically. Luke, however, tells us that the story begins not in the mystical beyond, but in the history of the whole human race. For Luke, the story of humankind and the story of salvation are one and the same. So there is a kind of double beginning to Luke's Gospel: the beginning of Jesus' actual life, a personal story that gets us involved in the central characters, and then a much longer view of where Jesus came from.

The first thing this tells us is that Luke sees salvation as a universal human issue—not limited by tribe or language, gender or education, wealth or poverty. It doesn't go back just to the prophets, or to the patriarchs, but right back to the very beginning of humanity, before there were any issues of human division to consider. 'Adam, the son of God' is the 'everyman', the type of humanity—so the gospel is for everyone.

Luke delivers on this promise as his Gospel unfolds. More than any of the other Gospel writers, he gives us the stories of the outcast and the marginalized, the women and the Gentiles, the ill and the maimed, the poor and the socially unacceptable. We meet the woman who bleeds, the girl who is dead, the centurion (who, of course, is the enemy), the leper and the demoniac who live outside the community for fear of contaminating the rest, and the Gentile woman who is an outsider. We hear the stories of the prodigal son who makes himself an outsider by eating pig food, and the lost sheep and lost coin, symbols of those who have been mislaid along the way. Luke traces the beginning of the gospel back to Adam, son of God, and then shows us that the gospel really is for everyone, even to the most ragged ends of society.

But there is a second theological point that we might construe from Luke's genealogy, which broadens out the whole meaning of salvation. By tracing the line right back to God himself, beyond the fall of humankind, to the perfection of the garden of Eden, Luke extends the story of salvation back to the beginning of everything. Without taking anything from the wonder of redemption, the story of Jesus' incarnation is more than merely a rescue plan for a world gone wrong. In Christian doctrine, salvation is something much more than just fixing or repairing a broken thing. The Latin word *salus* suggests the idea of wholeness, healing and completeness. Salvation carries no sense of disappointment, of a second-best option. In fact, it's about bringing something to full fruition. God becoming incarnate in Christ, then, is not just a rescue but a fulfilment of humanity; not merely a salve for a broken world but an expression of God's desire to reveal himself in such a way that we may become like him. It is interesting to wonder whether, if the world had always been perfect and the human race always existed in peace and harmony, there would have been any call for the story of Jesus at all. By taking the very beginning of humanity—'Adam, the son of God'—as the starting point of his Gospel, Luke suggests that perhaps there would.

[5 December]

Matthew: what's in a name?

An account of the genealogy of Jesus the Messiah, the son of David, the son of Abraham.

Abraham was the father of Isaac, and Isaac the father of Jacob, and Jacob the father of Judah and his brothers, and Judah the father of Perez and Zerah by Tamar, and Perez the father of Hezron, and Hezron the father of Aram, and Aram the father of Aminadab, and Aminadab the father of Nahshon, and Nahshon the father of Salmon, and Salmon the father of Boaz by Rahab, and Boaz the father of Obed by Ruth, and Obed the father of Jesse, and Jesse the father of King David.

And David was the father of Solomon by the wife of Uriah, and Solomon the father of Rehoboam, and Rehoboam the father of Abijah, and Abijah the father of Asaph, and Asaph the father of Jehoshaphat, and Jehoshaphat the father of Joram, and Joram the father of Uzziah, and Uzziah the father of Jotham, and Jotham the father of Ahaz, and Ahaz the father of Hezekiah, and Hezekiah the father of Manasseh, and Manasseh the father of Amos, and Amos the father of Josiah, and Josiah the father of Jechoniah and his brothers, at the time of the deportation to Babylon.

And after the deportation to Babylon: Jechoniah was the father of Salathiel, and Salathiel the father of Zerubbabel, and Zerubbabel the father of Abiud, and Abiud the father of Eliakim, and Eliakim the father of Azor, and Azor the father of Zadok, and Zadok the father of Achim, and Achim the father of Eliud, and Eliud the father of Eleazar, and Eleazar the father of Matthan, and Matthan the father of Jacob, and Jacob the father of Joseph the husband of Mary, of whom Jesus was born, who is called the Messiah.

So all the generations from Abraham to David are fourteen

generations; and from David to the deportation to Babylon, fourteen generations; and from the deportation to Babylon to the Messiah, fourteen generations.

MATTHEW 1:1–17

I promise you this is the last time I'm going to inflict lists of names on you! These lists feature more commonly in the Old Testament than the New, and they are sometimes nicknamed 'begats', because of the language of the King James Bible: 'Abraham begat Isaac, and Isaac begat Jacob', and so on. It's not often that we pause to consider these genealogies. For the most part, they seem to be the 'boring bits' of the Bible, but like most patterns, if you know what to look for, they do tell us something that's worth knowing.

I'm intrigued by the differences between Matthew's and Luke's accounts of Jesus' ancestors. Luke, the more natural storyteller of the two, starts with the story of Jesus' birth and then inserts the genealogy as a flashback, to give some context to the story, whereas Matthew wants all the technical and historical details in place from the start. To Matthew, the personal details of the birth stories are not very important: his concern is how the birth of Jesus changed the status of salvation history. Matthew tells us that the birth was announced, focusing on the angelic announcement and the fact that the prophecies were fulfilled. He then moves directly on to the story of the magi, which gives further detail to the symbolic significance of the birth of Jesus, but the personal details of the story are absent altogether. It may well be, of course, that Luke had access to personal stories and Matthew did not. All the same, Matthew writes more as if he is trying to prove a point about Jesus' significance as the inheritor and fulfiller of the ancient expectations and promises of a Messiah.

This difference in focus is reinforced by the fact that Matthew's and Luke's genealogies travel in opposite directions through time. Luke begins in the present and works backwards to show where Jesus came from. The beginning is viewed through the lens of the present, looking back to give some shape and context to the present but without detracting from the vibrancy of the focus on the present. Matthew, on the other hand, chooses a starting point back in history with the call of Abraham. Rather than going back to Adam, the son of God, as Luke did, Matthew describes Jesus as 'the son of David, the son of Abraham' (v. 1). His point is made by showing how the story of salvation connects up the dots between Abraham, David, the exile and the Messiah—the history of ancient Israel broken down into its major parts, and shown by Matthew to have perfect symmetry in its three divisions of 14 generations. He shows Jesus to be the true fulfilment of the messianic promises, because he is descended from Abraham, the great patriarch, and from David, the great king.

There's an interesting link between Matthew's genealogy and the first of the candles in an Advent wreath. Advent wreaths have either four or five candles in them (depending on where you come from). The four candles round the outside are either all red or three purple and one pink. These four candles are lit on the four successive Sundays of Advent, each symbolizing one character or group of characters who waited for the coming of the Messiah. In order, the candles represent the patriarchs, the prophets, John the Baptist and Mary, the mother of Jesus. Some wreaths also have a central white candle that is lit late on Christmas Eve to represent the Christ-child. Matthew's account of the salvation story traces it back to Abraham, to the promises of God to the patriarchs, and the establishment of God's covenant with Israel. To make sense of the new covenant, you have to start with the old covenant. In the coming days, we'll look at the beginning of the patriarchal journeys to the promised land, to see what the patriarchs can tell us about hearing the voice of God.

[6 December]

Mark: where the action is

The beginning of the good news of Jesus Christ, the Son of God. As it is written in the prophet Isaiah, 'See, I am sending my messenger ahead of you, who will prepare your way; the voice of one crying out in the wilderness: "Prepare the way of the Lord, make his paths straight"', John the baptizer appeared in the wilderness, proclaiming a baptism of repentance for the forgiveness of sins. And people from the whole Judean countryside and all the people of Jerusalem were going out to him, and were baptized by him in the river Jordan, confessing their sins. Now John was clothed with camel's hair, with a leather belt around his waist, and he ate locusts and wild honey. He proclaimed, 'The one who is more powerful than I is coming after me; I am not worthy to stoop down and untie the thong of his sandals. I have baptized you with water; but he will baptize you with the Holy Spirit.'

In those days Jesus came from Nazareth of Galilee and was baptized by John in the Jordan. And just as he was coming up out of the water, he saw the heavens torn apart and the Spirit descending like a dove on him. And a voice came from heaven, 'You are my Son, the Beloved; with you I am well pleased.'

MARK 1:1–11

While Luke and Matthew begin their Gospels with the birth stories, we see here that Mark starts with the adult Jesus. That's a reasonable shorthand description of the differences between the Gospels, and it's the primary reason that Mark doesn't get read much at Christmas. But where Mark chooses to begin the story is just as important and revealing as the narratives of the other Gospel writers.

Mark is obviously keen to get on with the action of the story. The first eight verses are the sum total of his preliminaries, and he then spends only another five verses on the baptism and temptations of Jesus before the story proper kicks off with the arrest of John the Baptist, which is the signal for the beginning of Jesus' ministry. A mere 13 verses of prologue, then, and Mark is right into the first act of his story.

Mark seems to address his Gospel to two big questions: 'Who is Jesus?' and 'What should a disciple of Jesus be like?' To answer his questions, though, he uses a writing style that is very immediate and pacy, almost journalistic. He uses the present and present continuous tenses a lot, which gives the feeling that the reader is right there in the story, watching the action, or perhaps that Mark himself is standing at the scene with a microphone, doing a TV commentary. There's no 'Once upon a time…' for Mark; he tells it right here, right now, often using phrases like 'And Jesus goes up the mountain…' or 'Now Jesus comes into the house, and says to them…' or 'And they bring him a blind man…'.

The fact that Mark's prologue is so brief makes it even more worthwhile to note that he doesn't begin the Gospel with Jesus but with John the Baptist, the herald of Christ, for whom the third candle in the Advent wreath is lit. The prophecy that Mark tells us comes from Isaiah is actually a mixture of Exodus 23:20, Isaiah 40:3 and Malachi 3:1. It's a mystery why he brought these three together, and highly unlikely that he made a mistake. It's perhaps worth noting that Malachi is the prophet who says specifically that Elijah will return before 'the great and terrible day of the Lord' (4:5–6), and John the Baptist is often seen as being a herald in the style and mode of Elijah. So perhaps Mark was calling on those words to strengthen the importance of John the Baptist in his narrative, although that still doesn't explain why he attributes the words to Isaiah alone.

Mark's starting point, then, is the prophets foretelling the herald who would announce the Messiah. However quickly he wants to turn to the immediacy of his main questions, 'Who is Jesus?' and 'What should we, his followers, be like?', he still anchors the story into the continuity between the ancient prophets and the contemporary herald of Christ.

In our generation, many hold the opinion that the Church is out of date and old-fashioned, and needs to do more to relate to the surrounding culture. There are all kinds of movements and groups that are concerned with this feeling. Many Christians have lost faith in the traditional denominations and have started up little groups that are trying to recreate Church without the institutional baggage. Within the denominations, there is a significant response to this loss of confidence in the Church, and various conversations and moves are afoot, such as the Anglican–Methodist move to support churches known as 'Fresh Expressions'. Conversations abound, around tables, on blogs and websites, about who and what the Church is. They are really asking the same big questions that Mark was asking—'Who is Jesus?' and 'What should we, his followers, be like?'—and they are approaching the questions with the same kind of immediacy and cut-to-the-chase attitude that Mark's writing portrays. It's worth noting, then, that even Mark thought it was important not to lose sight of the fact that every story grows out of somewhere, and he anchors his Gospel in with the 'big picture', connecting it to the prophets, the heralds, the enablers and the catalysts who brought the messianic vision into reality. It's important to get to the point and to find out what relevance it has for us, but there still has to be continuity with what went before.

[7 December]

Adam and Eve: the end of the beginning

They heard the sound of the Lord God walking in the garden at the time of the evening breeze, and the man and his wife hid themselves from the presence of the Lord God among the trees of the garden. But the Lord God called to the man, and said to him, 'Where are you?' He said, 'I heard the sound of you in the garden, and I was afraid, because I was naked; and I hid myself.' He said, 'Who told you that you were naked? Have you eaten from the tree of which I commanded you not to eat?' The man said, 'The woman whom you gave to be with me, she gave me fruit from the tree, and I ate.' Then the Lord God said to the woman, 'What is this that you have done?' The woman said, 'The serpent tricked me, and I ate.' The Lord God said to the serpent, 'Because you have done this, cursed are you among all animals and among all wild creatures; upon your belly you shall go, and dust you shall eat all the days of your life. I will put enmity between you and the woman, and between your offspring and hers; he will strike your head, and you will strike his heel.' To the woman he said, 'I will greatly increase your pangs in childbearing; in pain you shall bring forth children, yet your desire shall be for your husband, and he shall rule over you.' And to the man he said, 'Because you have listened to the voice of your wife, and have eaten of the tree about which I commanded you, "You shall not eat of it", cursed is the ground because of you; in toil you shall eat of it all the days of your life; thorns and thistles it shall bring forth for you; and you shall eat the plants of the field. By the sweat of your face you shall eat bread until you return to the ground, for out of it you were taken; you are dust, and to dust you shall return.'

GENESIS 3:8–19

In 1918, as the survivors of World War I began to return home and pick up their lives again, many found that their faith had taken too much of a beating for them simply to resume their churchgoing habits. For some, there was a realization that going to church had never, for them, been anything more than a social form. For others, their faith had formerly been based on the idea that Britain, still in empire mentality, had God's special approval, as if God was 'on our side'. This notion was blown to bits, along with tragic numbers of young lives, in the trenches of northern Europe. As the survivors returned, many discovered a complete loss of connection with the services and liturgies of the Church of England: words that had once seemed comforting and reassuring suddenly seemed alien, even quite offensive, in the light of their shattering wartime experiences.

It was in response to this that Eric Milner White, then Chaplain to King's College Cambridge, constructed the now famous Festival of Nine Lessons and Carols. He decided to abandon the structure of traditional liturgies for his Christmas service. Instead, he took an existing idea that had been used by E.W. Benson at Truro Cathedral and adapted it, choosing nine readings from the Bible that simply told the story of salvation and interspersing them with carols that illustrated the nine readings. His idea was that anyone, whether they were familiar with church doctrine or not, should be able to follow the story of salvation if it was told through these sequential readings and music. The Festival of Nine Lessons and Carols is still kept each Christmas Eve at King's College. Since 1928 it has been broadcast all over the world, and has become an important moment in the Christmas ritual for thousands of people. The first of the nine lessons is this account of Adam and Eve's 'fall from grace'. In Milner White's scheme, it forms the beginning of the salvation story by giving an account of the human condition and the need for salvation.

Few scholars now accept the idea of a single couple, created by God from the dust of the earth, as a literal account of history. Rather, the general view is that this is a story giving us an account of our relationship to God. The idea of sinless perfection and an unbroken, face-to-face relationship with God describes a fundamental religious longing, or a 'desire of the heart', as the psalmists might have put it. The idea that such an existence in Paradise was lost, and might again be restored, gives us a thoroughly human story: if you like, Adam and Eve are the 'everyman'. What matters is not whether they were literal historical figures, but that they describe for us the human dilemma of imperfection, guilt and broken relationship, and the longing for restoration.

Adam's reaction, when he hears God in the garden, is this: 'I hid myself' (v. 10). The most fundamental problem that lies behind the story of Christmas is the alienation of human beings from God. Why do we hide from God? Ever since the philosopher Kant redefined the self in terms of the subject and the object, we have identified ourselves in terms of the self as distinct from the 'other' —and when it comes to talking about God, there is no one more 'other' than he is. However aware we are that we are separate and alien from one another, we are even more so by comparison to God. God is morally 'other'—however good we are, we never match his perfection; he is physically 'other'—he doesn't grow old or suffer from backache or toothache, and he isn't limited by space or gravity. God is 'other' in the field of knowledge also: I cannot tell him anything he doesn't know already.

We are, of course, able to overcome our problem of interpersonal alienation to a certain degree. Even though we are aware of our separation from one another, we do form close connections, even to the extent of finding a soulmate—someone who, despite being 'other', somehow seems to fit perfectly with me, to understand me without effort, to have some kind of mystical connection to me, to hold the key to the door of my soul, the password to my internal files. Such relationships give us a glimpse of how life might be were we not alienated from others and from God.

Preparing the ground for the Christmas story, then, this passage sets out for us what our situation is: we know that we should be at peace with ourselves and closely connected with one another and with God, and yet we find ourselves alienated and unable to maintain an intimate connection either with God (v. 10) or with each other (v. 15). We are divided from each other, often over the smallest things. As the medieval carol, 'Adam lay ybounden', puts it so eloquently, 'And all was for an apple, an apple that he took.' For the sake of this apple, Adam proceeded to 'shop' his wife (v. 12). It is not difficult to imagine Eve's outrage. To be blamed for a wrongdoing by the person who was responsible is a serious betrayal; when that betrayal comes from a spouse, the damage goes very deep indeed.

So the first of Milner White's Nine Lessons lays out the problem: we are alienated from one another and alienated from God. Something or someone needs to break the deadlock. Someone needs to make the circumstances possible—to bring these alienated beings into each other's orbit, so that they can discover themselves in one another.

[SECTION 2]

In between: patriarchs and promises

The first candle on an Advent wreath is lit to represent the patriarchs. Abraham heard God's call and set out to find the promised land. His descendants began to live in the land of Canaan, gradually refining their understanding of the promise. Over the next few days, we'll look at the patriarchs, considering how they heard God's call and what it meant for them to begin new journeys or to live during 'in-between' times.

[8 December]

Abraham's call

Terah took his son Abram and his grandson Lot son of Haran, and his daughter-in-law Sarai, his son Abram's wife, and they went out together from Ur of the Chaldeans to go into the land of Canaan; but when they came to Haran, they settled there. The days of Terah were two hundred and five years; and Terah died in Haran.

Now the Lord said to Abram, 'Go from your country and your kindred and your father's house to the land that I will show you. I will make of you a great nation, and I will bless you, and make your name great, so that you will be a blessing. I will bless those who bless you, and the one who curses you I will curse; and in you all the families of the earth shall be blessed.' So Abram went, as the Lord had told him; and Lot went with him. Abram was seventy-five years old when he departed from Haran. Abram took his wife Sarai and his brother's son Lot, and all the possessions that they had gathered, and the persons whom they had acquired in Haran; and they set forth to go to the land of Canaan.

GENESIS 11:31—12:5

We noted earlier that Matthew tells the story of salvation beginning with the patriarchs, who are always remembered on the first Sunday in Advent by the lighting of the first candle on the Advent wreath. The patriarchs were the families who set out on a nomadic journey through the plains of the Middle East towards the promised land, and their story starts with the passage we have just read about the call of Abram (later renamed Abraham).

This account of God's call to Abram is, of course, given to us from a retrospective point of view, and telling the story after the event always makes things seem clearer than they were at the time.

It appears from this account that God spoke audibly and unmistakably to Abram, yet the experience of life and the unfolding of the story in the subsequent chapters suggest that this was unlikely. It is just as possible that Abram 'heard' God's call in the same way we do—little by little, over time, as a growing sense deep inside that a particular direction or course of action is the one we must take.

We sometimes operate from a very limited idea of what a call from God might be, believing that a call is only to a specific Christian ministry, that a call is unmistakable and clear, and that it will take us in a new and different direction that bears no relationship to where we were before. Abram's story doesn't really follow this pattern, though, and the story of his call 'debunks' some popular misconceptions about what it means to hear a call from God.

We may limit our idea of what a call is by believing that we need to have a clear vision of the end from the beginning, but it's often the case that when people begin to sense God's Spirit leading them into new things, the destination or the end result of that call is somewhat vague and subject to revision. In discerning God's call, it seems to be far less important to be certain where the call is taking you than to sense that God is beginning something and that you have to get up and begin to follow. Abram's call from God included only the vaguest detail as to where he would end up: all he had was the promise that God would show him later where he was going (12:1); he was called to begin the journey without knowing his destination. What Abram did have, though, was a clear sense of direction and purpose, and a conviction that it was God who had called him and would guide him along the way. Journeying with God usually means not knowing from the start what the end will be. In fact, if Abram's story is anything to go by, the idea of the destination is likely to be revised and expanded as the journey continues.

We sometimes limit our idea of what a call is by assuming it must be something radical, new and unexpected. Yet here we see that even something as important as the call of Abram didn't come out of nowhere: 'They went out together from Ur of the Chaldeans to go into the land of Canaan; but when they came to Haran, they settled there' (11:31). Abram's call from God involved picking up an old vision that had got lost along the way; it had a continuity with where he had come from. Why an old vision? It's impossible to tell: maybe the family had felt this call from God before, or perhaps, when Abram sensed it was time to move, the extent of his imagination was what was already planted in his mind: he had been on the way to Canaan with his father's family when they 'stopped at Haran'. God does not always breathe new and unthought of ideas into our minds. Far more often, he takes the direction of our life as it is and calls us to re-imagine it into a new shape. Neither did the new call involve leaving everything else behind. Certainly Abram had to leave Haran behind, but he took with him his entire family, including the nephew who had become part of his household and all his possessions. The call of God seems to involve choosing what to take and what to leave behind and the willingness to do the sorting out and packing up that makes moving possible.

We also limit our idea of what a call is by imagining that it is always good news—something joyful and exciting. A new beginning nearly always involves the ending of something else. Sometimes, what makes way for a new sense of call is a life-changing event. A death, a child leaving home, a marriage breakdown or a forced career change such as a redundancy—these are the kinds of unsought traumas that open up the possibility of change for us. The ending that makes way for a new beginning may be painful, and a new sense of calling might involve grieving before rejoicing. We may have to deal with the darkness of bereavement or the fear and insecurity of a change in financial circumstances, before the way forward opens up in hope. The beginning of Abram's call was the death of his father. But somehow, as he emerged from grief, rather than settling down again, Abram opened up to the possibility of new things and a hopeful future.

A call, then, is more a sense of direction and purpose than a clear vision of the future; it is a hunch that there is something beyond the horizon that deserves to be found, together with the belief that God will guide us along the way and that, ultimately, he will bless us and make the journey worthwhile.

Abram had two qualities that enabled him to follow God. The first was the willingness to leave his comfort zone behind, to go to all the trouble of packing up and moving. The second quality, though, was what gave him the energy for all that packing and sorting and moving: the capacity to imagine, dream, hope for a new world and a bigger life. This is where the beginning of the story of salvation lies.

[9 December]

Land and promise

Abram took his wife Sarai and his brother's son Lot, and all the possessions that they had gathered, and the persons whom they had acquired in Haran; and they set forth to go to the land of Canaan. When they had come to the land of Canaan, Abram passed through the land to the place at Shechem, to the oak of Moreh. At that time the Canaanites were in the land. Then the Lord appeared to Abram, and said, 'To your offspring I will give this land.' So he built there an altar to the Lord, who had appeared to him. From there he moved on to the hill country on the east of Bethel, and pitched his tent, with Bethel on the west and Ai on the east; and there he built an altar to the Lord and invoked the name of the Lord. And Abram journeyed on by stages towards the Negeb.

GENESIS 12:5–9

We read yesterday that Abram's call was clear about the beginning of the journey, but vague about the destination. The one detail Abram did have, though, was that the destination was a place—'a land that I will show you' (12:1). As the story of the patriarchs develops in the early Old Testament stories, we read over and over again that they were increasingly caught up in this quest for a place. Their hopes of redemption, their hopes of a better life and of the blessings of God, gradually became more and more focused on the place: the land of promise.

It's interesting to notice, then, that when Abram first arrives in Canaan and God confirms his promise, Abram is in no hurry to build a city and settle down. Wherever he stops, he builds an altar and worships God, but then continues to travel about. His arrival in the promised land did not alter the fact that Abraham was a nomad and continued to live as one. His call was to discover a land, but not immediately to become a settled community.

Among the tribes that eventually gelled together to form the nation of ancient Israel were many groups of nomads. Nomads are not rootless wanderers. They live within large areas of land, keeping livestock in complex climatic conditions and moving with the seasons to put their herds on to the best pastures. They constantly return to the same places, pitching camp and staying until the weather or the pasture moves them on again. They return season by season to old pasturing places, uncovering wells that they have dug before.

Often, we use Old Testament stories to reflect on the idea of leaving our clutter behind in order to follow God, but the truth of the nomadic life is that not much clutter is accumulated, and it's *de rigueur*, when you move, to take all your stuff with you. When Abram left Ur of the Chaldees, he packed up all his possessions and took his entire household with him. Our culture of consumerism makes us very bad indeed at cleaning up; we tend to treat everything as disposable and create mountains of rubbish wherever we live. Perhaps, rather than drawing lessons from Abram about leaving things behind, we might think about taking responsibility for our clutter and for the impact of our presence upon the space we occupy.

Despite the fact that the patriarchal journey was intricately woven together with a quest for land, the promise always seems to keep Abram moving forward. Maybe in that there is an image for us: that wherever we have been and wherever we are at present, it is both normal and desirable still to see something more beyond the horizon. The journey into God is a journey that is constantly closer, often following paths that we have trodden before, but—if it is God we are encountering—we can never completely lay hold of what we seek, and the journey, once begun, is always in process. Every arrival seems like an ending but, in fact, it is a pause before the next beginning. The journey into God is not rootless but, like Abraham, we need to keep a nomadic sense of mobility.

Although the promised land is an iconic feature of the patriarchal stories, owning and controlling the land comes only at a later stage in the Old Testament narratives. At this point in the story, Abraham is grateful to God for what the land offers, yet he also continues to observe nomadic etiquette, including the unwritten law that you cannot over-occupy pasture. Later in Genesis, we read of Abram and Lot splitting up to spread their growing flocks over a larger area. Fighting over land, for nomadic tribes, is counterproductive and self-defeating.

So, having found and acknowledged the promised land, Abram worships and then moves on. As he continues to move, he discovers that the land of promise is very large indeed. He pauses at all the places to which his descendants will later return. This land, then, is one that (with the benefit of a nomadic mindset) can be shared respectfully with neighbouring tribes; it also has expandable borders. If Abram had set a boundary around that first plot of land and fought the Canaanites, the land of promise would have been much smaller. As it was, the promise was more loosely associated with boundaries in these early narratives than was later the case, when ancient Israel shifted in their mode of life from being nomads to being settlers.

We might remember, too, that the promise (which we read yesterday) was only partly to do with the land. From Abram's point of view, the focus was not, first and foremost, on owning and occupying the land but on having heirs. So, although the patriarchs are powerfully associated with the journey to the land of promise, the very first person to arrive there already realized that the land itself was not the sum total of what it was all about.

Present-day conflict in the Middle East is still fuelled by connections between religious inheritance and land, and we might pray for a return to a looser association between these things. Meantime, in our personal lives, we might ask ourselves what we are powerfully attached to as an idea of promise. Is it an idea that needs disentangling in order for us to discover what our true priorities should be?

[10 December]

Redigging the wells

Isaac... camped in the valley of Gerar and settled there. Isaac dug again the wells of water that had been dug in the days of his father Abraham; for the Philistines had stopped them up after the death of Abraham; and he gave them the names that his father had given them. But when Isaac's servants dug in the valley and found there a well of spring water, the herders of Gerar quarrelled with Isaac's herders, saying, 'The water is ours.' So he called the well Esek, because they contended with him. Then they dug another well, and they quarrelled over that one also; so he called it Sitnah. He moved from there and dug another well, and they did not quarrel over it; so he called it Rehoboth, saying, 'Now the Lord has made room for us, and we shall be fruitful in the land.'

From there he went up to Beer-sheba. And that very night the Lord appeared to him and said, 'I am the God of your father Abraham; do not be afraid, for I am with you and will bless you and make your offspring numerous for my servant Abraham's sake.' So he built an altar there, called on the name of the Lord, and pitched his tent there. And there Isaac's servants dug a well. Then Abimelech went to him from Gerar, with Ahuzzath his adviser and Phicol the commander of his army. Isaac said to them, 'Why have you come to me, seeing that you hate me and have sent me away from you?' They said, 'We see plainly that the Lord has been with you; so we say, let there be an oath between you and us, and let us make a covenant with you so that you will do us no harm, just as we have not touched you and have done to you nothing but good and have sent you away in peace. You are now the blessed of the Lord.' So he made them a feast, and they ate and drank. In the morning they rose early and exchanged oaths; and Isaac set them on their way, and they departed from him in peace. That same day Isaac's servants came and told him about the well that they had dug, and said to him, 'We have found water!' He called it Shibah; therefore the name of the city is Beer-sheba to this day.

GENESIS 26:17–33

We have already seen from the journeys of Abraham that the patriarchs were nomadic people, and when they first lived in the land of promise, they did so as nomads, moving around to follow the pastures. As they went, they built a trail of wells and desert altars, some of which you can still see today in the archeological sites in the southern, desert areas of Israel.

It's no surprise, then, to read about Isaac returning to an old pasturing site and redigging one of Abraham's wells, but here Isaac ran into conflict with some Philistines who were pasturing their flocks on land nearby. The Philistines, it is thought, were not natives of the land but incomers from across a stretch of sea. They had no more claim to the land than Isaac did, but it seemed that they were willing to put up a fight for the land once Isaac had found that most precious of commodities—water.

Isaac, though, was not looking for a fight. He gave them the well and moved on. A second time he was challenged, and a second time he gave up his well, preferring to keep moving than to get into a fight. He continued to circle round these hostile neighbours until, at the third attempt, he found pastures and water that they did not want. In the midst of all this well-digging, Isaac had a first-hand experience of God, and God reiterated to Isaac the promises that had first been made to his father, Abraham. Then, apparently noticing that Isaac had not been scared away and was successful at every attempt to dig for water, Abimelech, the king of the Philistines, sought to make a peace treaty with Isaac.

What are we to make of this ancient story of well-digging and altar-building in the midst of hostile neighbours? I think there are two lessons we could draw from Isaac's experiences.

The first is a lesson about being an in-between generation.

Abram's descendants continued their nomadic existence for several generations before they eventually settled and occupied the land of promise. Whole generations, like Isaac's, were the in-between generations. They didn't see the beginning of the journey and they didn't see the end of it. They were like the middle runners in a relay race, getting neither the starter's orders nor the glory of the finishing tape. Their job was to pick up the vision, carry it on and then hand it over to the next generation.

Perhaps our generation of the Church is something like this. Thousands of generations into a long line of relay runners, we sometimes feel like giving up the race. Advent focuses us on both the first coming of Christ in the flesh and his second coming in the future. Yet, the first coming is now very far away, and living as we do in an era often described as post-Christian, the promise of a second coming is ever more difficult to comprehend. The glorious days of Christendom are a fading dream and we constantly hear about the demise of the Church, the death of Christian culture and the incredibility of Christian belief. We are far from the beginning of the journey, and we have no clear sight of a triumphant end. How tempting to believe that it will all just fizzle out! And it would be so easy to give up and allow ourselves to be assumed into the surrounding culture.

Isaac might be able to teach us something here. He didn't pick a fight with the surrounding culture, but neither did he allow it to subsume him. He continued to dig in all the places his father had taught him until he found a place that he could peacefully occupy, a place that his hostile neighbours did not steal from him. He didn't claim any right to the land but inwardly he refused to give up on the promise God had made to Abram, despite the fact that, for Isaac, it was a second-hand promise.

One of the temptations of living in a post-Christian culture is to attempt to recreate the Church from scratch. A loss of faith in the traditions of the Church lead many to abandon the tradition and begin, as it were, to dig for water in new places. In Isaac's story, we have a picture of someone who goes back to the traditional sources and begins to dig for himself. He doesn't rest on his father's laurels; neither does he set out for a new land. He finds the traditional sites and then he digs.

The result, for Isaac, was that in the end he heard God's promise for himself. He worked within the beliefs and traditions he'd inherited from his father until the second-hand promise became a first-hand encounter with God.

The second lesson is, perhaps, a surprising one, but certainly a welcome find among ancient stories that are sometimes used as political dynamite. We read here that although Isaac believed himself to be journeying into a land of promise, he discovered that a covenant with God can be a socially integrating force, not one that forces us into a ghetto. Holding on to God's promises does not mean that we have to become enemies with those who do not share our point of view. God's promise of blessing need not be at the expense of others. There is room in the world—even (especially) in the place of promise—for others who do not share our view of the world. The blessing is not narrow and it does not have to lead us into a combative mindset. Isaac's philosophical response when he finally found land that his hostile neighbours did not challenge was one of gratitude: 'the Lord has made room for us' (v. 22). But he did not expect God to make room for him by wiping out his neighbours; rather, he continued to search until he found a peaceable solution.

Isaac's approach to conflict resolution may seem too soft to some. Was he too much of a pushover? Should he have stood up for himself against these incomers who, after all, had no more right to the land than he did? But the end result speaks volumes: his refusal to run away, his willingness to persevere, his willingness to share the water he found, won his neighbours in the end.

The covenant with God, then, did not lead Isaac to assume that he had a right to lord it over other contenders for the land, and, in the end, the covenant with God led to a covenant with Isaac's neighbours. It would be naïve to think that politics could always be that simple, and we know that later events in the Old Testament tell a different story. Nevertheless, this story clearly lays out the possibility that a promise from God might be shared with awkward neighbours of entirely different viewpoints.

[SECTION 3]

Prophets and heralds

The second candle on the Advent wreath is lit to remember the prophets, who announced the coming of the Lord. Most of the messianic prophecies are found with the group of prophets known as the eighth-century prophets.

Mark's Gospel began with the announcement of the prophets and of John the Baptist. John the Baptist is an important figure in Advent: he is the focus of the third Sunday of Advent, for whom we light the third candle on the Advent wreath. His announcement of the kingdom shifts the gear of Advent meditations from looking inward and backwards reflectively on our history, to looking forward to the immediacy of God's presence breaking into our world and our lives. By tradition, John the Baptist has the spirit of the prophet Elijah, and we will look here at Elijah as the first of our prophets, and as the model for John.

[11 December]

Calling down fire: who's setting the agenda?

So Ahab sent to all the Israelites, and assembled the prophets at Mount Carmel. Elijah then came near to all the people, and said, 'How long will you go limping with two different opinions? If the Lord is God, follow him; but if Baal, then follow him.' The people did not answer him a word. Then Elijah said to the people, 'I, even I only, am left a prophet of the Lord; but Baal's prophets number four hundred and fifty. Let two bulls be given to us; let them choose one bull for themselves, cut it in pieces, and lay it on the wood, but put no fire to it; I will prepare the other bull and lay it on the wood, but put no fire to it. Then you call on the name of your god and I will call on the name of the Lord; the god who answers by fire is indeed God.' All the people answered, 'Well spoken!' ...

[Elijah] built an altar in the name of the Lord. Then he made a trench around the altar, large enough to contain two measures of seed. Next he put the wood in order, cut the bull in pieces, and laid it on the wood. He said, 'Fill four jars with water and pour it on the burnt-offering and on the wood.' Then he said, 'Do it a second time'; and they did it a second time. Again he said, 'Do it a third time'; and they did it a third time, so that the water ran all round the altar, and filled the trench also with water. At the time of the offering of the oblation, the prophet Elijah came near and said, 'O Lord, God of Abraham, Isaac, and Israel, let it be known this day that you are God in Israel, that I am your servant, and that I have done all these things at your bidding. Answer me, O Lord, answer me, so that this people may know that you, O Lord, are God, and that you have turned their hearts back.' Then the fire of the Lord fell and consumed the burnt-offering,

the wood, the stones, and the dust, and even licked up the water that was in the trench. When all the people saw it, they fell on their faces and said, 'The Lord indeed is God; the Lord indeed is God.'

1 KINGS 18:20–24, 32–39

Elijah is an important figure in the background of the Advent stories because he is the 'type' (or foreshadowing) of John the Baptist. What kind of person could be a herald of Christ? A circumspect, scholarly type who thinks before they speak, always sees both sides of the argument and reasons out an intellectual understanding of the Christ? No, that kind of person would certainly be wise, and might qualify as one of the Magi, but not as a herald. A quiet, thoughtful person who would say nothing in public but would germinate the work of God in private contemplative prayer? Probably not. That sort of person would make a wonderful mother of Christ, but not a great herald. A herald has to be a risk taker, someone who will speak out fearlessly, put their money where their mouth is and let their actions, clothes, lifestyle and public image speak for them. That's what John the Baptist would need to be when he arrived on the scene—and the role model the prophets chose? Elijah.

Elijah is one of my favourite characters in the Bible. He is full of energy and passion, a man who cares about truth and about the honour of God, and gets thoroughly involved in the world he lives in. There's no hiding away at the prayer meeting for Elijah. But it's impossible to make great big public statements about faith or God through actions or words without occasionally making an equally great big and public mistake. A man like Elijah, if he was going to make a mistake, would be bound to do so to dramatic effect. I love his mistakes as much as his successes, though: our weaknesses are usually the flipside of our strengths, and I hold to the adage that it's better to make a few mistakes than never make anything at all.

Elijah's showdown with the prophets of Baal on the mountainside is often understood in terms of its success in demonstrating the power of God. But if you look at it from a different angle, it can equally be construed as quite a hollow triumph. It reads to me like an essay on who sets the agenda. Most of Elijah's prophetic actions up to this point have been preceded by a phrase like 'The word of the Lord came to Elijah…', but not this time. Elijah had spent years of his life trying to persuade people to take God seriously. Looking around his community, he was aggrieved to see how fickle people were in their beliefs. They were fair-weather believers, easily won over to an alternative point of view. Their faith was so shallow that they would quickly abandon it in favour of the latest popular idea, or whatever would give them success. The inspiration for Elijah's challenge to the Baal worshippers on the hillside was not 'the word of the Lord', but the faithlessness of his people, the threats of a cruel and ruthless king and the taunts of those who mocked Elijah's God.

It's all too easy to allow other people's challenges to our faith to set the agenda for us. Whenever some debate about religion and science, or religion and ethics, or religion and whatever, hits the headlines, we sometimes get drawn in, not because it's a debate worth having but because we are afraid that people will think our faith is out of date, intellectually unreasonable or not very well thought through. It's so easy to jump to the defence and spend time and effort presenting our point of view, our faith, as a credible alternative to the popular one that taunts us from the booklists and the headlines. If our social standing is at stake, or our livelihood or, in more extreme circumstances, our own safety, then a desperation can grow in us to prove that our faith is credible, true, worthwhile—partly for God's sake but also for our own. If our defence of faith is motivated by fear, though, especially fear of a shallow, populist debate, it's a defence not worth making. If we rise to that kind of bait, we do what Elijah did on the mountainside. We lose our perspective, begin to believe that we alone are defending the truth, overestimate the power of the challenge, and underestimate how many other people see the flaws in the popular view.

Elijah began to think he was the only one left who was faithful to the Lord, yet we learn later in the story (19:18) that in fact there were 7000 others—quite a lot in the ancient world! What was

Elijah doing on Mount Carmel? Was he concerned only with God's honour, or was he in a tailspin of insecurity about his own faith? We cannot ignore, of course, the fact that God did send the fire for Elijah, and this in itself is an interesting phenomenon. God did not 'hold out' on Elijah: he gave him what he needed in the moment. Perhaps there was some purpose in that, either for Elijah or the worshippers of Baal, or the downtrodden and insecure worshippers of God. Yet, as we shall see, although God sent the fire, once God really had Elijah's ear, Elijah found that God was not in the fire (19:12).

When contemporary debates demand that we prove that God is real, or that our God is not a delusion, outdated or displaced by science, what should we do? Should we, metaphorically speaking, rush to build an altar, pour on water and call down fire to prove that we are right? It's important to engage with contemporary debates and to be thoroughly involved in our world and our culture. We also need to pay attention to how we and our God are perceived in the world. There's also a place for listening thoughtfully to genuine challenges to our beliefs. But there's a difference between engaging with genuine argument and allowing the latest popular media fad to set the agenda for us.

Last time a popular book was published claiming that religion was the cause of all the ills in the world and that science made belief in God no longer viable, I began to find that conversation over lunch and coffee, and on websites and blogs, demanded more and more response to something that I simply found theologically vacuous. A number of people told me that now the Christian faith had been challenged, I ought to write a book in response to prove that my faith was true. I decided simply not to get involved in those conversations. I had a lot of important work going on, which would not get done if I spent my mental and emotional energy on some-one else's agenda, so I resolved that I would only discuss the issue as time allowed, with people who were genuinely interested and not just wanting to indulge in Christian-baiting.

I'm glad I pulled back. I got my work done and published and, by setting limits on my involvement in that conversation, I stayed relaxed and untroubled by the invective that was flying elsewhere. Then one day I fell into conversation with a pronounced atheist whom I have known for years, who asked why I hadn't engaged with the debate publicly. I explained that I felt the whole thing was a distraction and was attacking a God that I didn't actually believe in. Suddenly it was as if the penny dropped for my friend. 'You mean, the God I keep trying to disprove to you, you don't even believe in?' he said. 'Yup,' I said. 'So what do you believe in, then?' he asked. The refusal to get into a fight meant that one person, at least, suddenly saw that the conflict was of no consequence. We were talking about different things. It was as if a light went on in his eyes, and he said, 'Well, if that's what you mean by God, then I think I might have more in common with you than I ever realized...'

The challenges that come our way may be worthwhile, but equally they may be distractions. If, as Elijah did with the Baal worshippers, we let others set the agenda for us, we may waste our energy arguing with people who are not listening when we could be doing something far more valuable. Even if we win the argument, as Elijah did, we might then find ourselves spiritually and mentally exhausted without really having achieved a great deal. Not every demand to prove God in contemporary debate is a call from God. We are not obliged to defend God at the whim of others. We should be sure that we listen to the wisdom of God and choose carefully where we pour out our precious time and energy.

[12 December]

Eat, drink, sleep

Ahab told Jezebel all that Elijah had done, and how he had killed all the prophets with the sword. Then Jezebel sent a messenger to Elijah, saying, 'So may the gods do to me, and more also, if I do not make your life like the life of one of them by this time tomorrow.' Then he was afraid; he got up and fled for his life, and came to Beer-sheba, which belongs to Judah; he left his servant there.

But he himself went a day's journey into the wilderness, and came and sat down under a solitary broom tree. He asked that he might die: 'It is enough; now, O Lord, take away my life, for I am no better than my ancestors.' Then he lay down under the broom tree and fell asleep. Suddenly an angel touched him and said to him, 'Get up and eat.' He looked, and there at his head was a cake baked on hot stones, and a jar of water. He ate and drank, and lay down again. The angel of the Lord came a second time, touched him, and said, 'Get up and eat, otherwise the journey will be too much for you.' He got up, and ate and drank; then he went in the strength of that food for forty days and forty nights to Horeb the mount of God. At that place he came to a cave, and spent the night there.

1 KINGS 19:1–9A

The prophets who have whole books named after them came mostly from around the eighth century BC, and were renowned for their words, for perceiving the signs of the times and writing down their warnings of disaster and predictions of future hope. Elijah, though, was from an earlier school of prophets, who were renowned not so much for memorable poetic words as for living in small communities that embodied their prophetic message through their lifestyle and their actions. The great messianic prophecies come from the later prophets, but these earlier prophets do, nonetheless, have something to tell us about the anticipation of the coming Messiah. Not least is Elijah, often described as the greatest of the prophets, yet whose young protegé Elisha, when he inherited Elijah's mantle, in some ways surpassed Elijah's prophetic acts. In this, too, we might see a foreshadowing of the relationship between John the Baptist and Jesus—John who said, 'After me One is coming who is mightier than I...' (Mark 1:7, NASB). Both Elijah and John understood that true greatness, for a prophet, is to point towards something, someone, greater than themselves.

Yesterday we read about Elijah's attempt to prove that his God was the true God on Mount Carmel. After the grand demonstration of power had shown that he was right, you might expect him to be feeling triumphant, walking on air. But, as I have suggested, the triumph was a hollow one: the anticlimax brought Elijah very low and his confidence deserted him. He had reason to be afraid for his life, given that Jezebel would cheerfully have murdered Elijah for crossing her. For some reason, Elijah trusted God to send down fire miraculously but not to protect him from Jezebel's bullying threats, and so he fled for his life.

But the desert, his hiding place, was precisely where God met him and restored him, body and soul. The famous and memorable parts of this chapter in Elijah's life are the fire on Mount Carmel and the cave where he heard the 'still, small voice'. In between Mount Carmel and the cave, though, is one of the most poignant accounts in the Old Testament histories, for it was here in the desert that Elijah finally collapsed, completely exhausted and in absolute despair. Here God met him in his most profound moment of need and gave him the most basic practical human care: food, drink and sleep.

How often we imagine that we must get ourselves to the place where we can hear God! 'If I could only find a free day, a spare weekend, a clear hour, to read and think and re-evaluate, perhaps then God would speak to me. Perhaps then I would gain some perspective on life.' But the gear change that comes to Elijah's relationship with God happens here in the middle of the desert. Back on Mount Carmel, it seems to have been Elijah's great faith that won the day. All too often, we hear that it is our faith that is the issue. 'God will be able to act if I have enough faith, if I pray often enough, if I pray in the right way, if I believe the right set of things. Then God will act.' But this approach to faith puts the emphasis on the individual. Who is it who is about to act? Is it God? Or is it me? Is God so small that he cannot act, or so mean that he will not, unless I pray in just the right way or have the right amount of faith?

Elijah's act of faith on the Mount Carmel certainly brought down fire from heaven. Later, though, in the cave, he discovers that God is not in the fire. It may be that God can be cajoled into speaking through fire, but it seems that this is not God's preferred method of communication. God is not in the wind or the earthquake or the fire, or any other dramatic mode of power. God speaks in stillness and quiet; God speaks in the depth of our hearts.

Between the fire on the mountainside and the still small voice in the cave, Elijah has to go through a shift of perspective, a change of heart. Out in the desert, he collapses in the middle of nowhere, as people often do when they exhaust themselves by depending on their faith rather than on God. And out in the middle of nowhere is the place where, at last, God is able to reach him. In the end, it is not Elijah who gets himself to the place where he can hear God, but God himself.

Perhaps the loveliest thing of all about this story is the way in which God helps Elijah to reach the place where he can hear God's voice. If you were in need of a spiritual revelation, what would you do to prepare yourself? Pray? Go on a retreat? What Elijah needed in preparation was not a 40-day fast or a course in biblical interpretation. What he needed first—and what God provided—were the basic physical necessities: food, water and sleep.

The things we need before we can hear God speaking to us are often not anything to do with spiritual preparations. God is, perhaps, not the stoic we imagine: given that he was a God who expressed himself most fully in incarnation, in flesh and blood, we should not be surprised by this. Yet we are so slow to believe that it is right within our own humanity that God meets us.

Eat, drink and sleep. Not eat, drink and be merry, mind you: this is not a mandate for careless hedonism but a recognition that the human mind and body do not function well on sleep deprivation, dehydration and poor nutrition.

As a College Chaplain in a highly competitive university, I often find myself talking to students who come under huge stress about work and exams. There are many ways to tackle stress, and psychological and spiritual understanding certainly play their part, as do basic time management skills. More often than not, though, as I talk through the causes of stress with my students, I find that they are working through the small hours of the night, skipping meals and sleep, and then going out drinking in order to relax. No wonder they are stressed! My top recommendation to them is not to pray or to work harder, but to eat and sleep, stay off the alcohol for a few days and drink lots of water.

Life out of kilter? Need to find God afresh? Eat, drink, sleep. Don't forget that you are a body as well as a soul. The still, small voice is hard to hear when your body is exhausted and you are sleep-deprived. Increase your chances of hearing that voice by looking after yourself—body and soul.

[13 December]

Not in the fire…

[Elijah] came to a cave, and spent the night there. Then the word of the Lord came to him, saying, 'What are you doing here, Elijah?' He answered, 'I have been very zealous for the Lord, the God of hosts; for the Israelites have forsaken your covenant, thrown down your altars, and killed your prophets with the sword. I alone am left, and they are seeking my life, to take it away.'

He said, 'Go out and stand on the mountain before the Lord, for the Lord is about to pass by.' Now there was a great wind, so strong that it was splitting mountains and breaking rocks in pieces before the Lord, but the Lord was not in the wind; and after the wind an earthquake, but the Lord was not in the earthquake; and after the earthquake a fire, but the Lord was not in the fire; and after the fire a sound of sheer silence. When Elijah heard it, he wrapped his face in his mantle and went out and stood at the entrance of the cave. Then there came a voice to him that said, 'What are you doing here, Elijah?' He answered, 'I have been very zealous for the Lord, the God of hosts; for the Israelites have forsaken your covenant, thrown down your altars, and killed your prophets with the sword. I alone am left, and they are seeking my life, to take it away.' Then the Lord said to him, 'Go, return on your way to the wilderness of Damascus; when you arrive, you shall anoint Hazael as king over Aram. Also you shall anoint Jehu son of Nimshi as king over Israel; and you shall anoint Elisha son of Shaphat of Abel-meholah as prophet in your place. Whoever escapes from the sword of Hazael, Jehu shall kill; and whoever escapes from the sword of Jehu, Elisha shall kill. Yet I will leave seven thousand in Israel, all the knees that have not bowed to Baal, and every mouth that has not kissed him.'

1 KINGS 19:9–18

Over the last two days, we have read how Elijah attempted to prove that his God was the true God by calling down fire from heaven, and immediately found that this did not make him a triumphant prophet but an exhausted and burnt-out minister, with a failure of nerve and a loss of perspective. Knowing that, at the moment of extreme weakness, God gave Elijah not a sharp spiritual lesson but food, drink and sleep is enough to reduce any burnt-out minister to tears. People who burn out in their faith are often perfectionists, people who work far too hard for the cause and people who, when they find that 150 per cent isn't enough, expect to be told they must work harder. God, though, is clearly more in favour of ordinary humanity than we dare believe.

Only when Elijah has begun to recover physically and mentally is he able to contemplate the events of the previous weeks and ask where God was in them all. What is amazing to read here is that God was not in the wind or the earthquake—and not only that, but God was *not in the fire*. Elijah surely couldn't have failed to make the connection with his great 'triumph' on the mountainside. God sent the fire. He vindicated Elijah, and yet God was not in the fire. It is not God's preferred method of communication to produce a dramatic miracle to settle a conflict. How does God communicate? In a still, small voice—less than an inaudible whisper—a 'sound of sheer silence', as NRSV translates verse 12.

When we are trying to be superhuman, living at such a pace and volume that we cannot hear God unless he shouts, he will sometimes send down the fire. When we are so burnt out that we cannot help ourselves, he will sometimes send an angel to compel us to be simply human again. But we will never hear God for ourselves until we slow down, make time to eat and drink and sleep, stop isolating ourselves so that we are trapped into thinking we are alone and indispensable, and create enough still points in our lives that we can hear the voice in the stillness.

The second point that catches my eye in today's reading is the instruction from God to anoint Elisha 'as prophet in your place' (v. 16). I remember, years ago, suffering no small anxiety from hearing this phrase interpreted as a threat of condemnation, and as a threat that failing to carry out God's commands or running away from God's call would result in a second-best life. Years later, having learnt a few things about the love, grace and patience of God, experience leads me to question this interpretation. Looking more closely, I have found that the biblical narrative doesn't support such a draconian view either. Why? Well, Elijah did continue in his ministry, and an important part of it was teaching Elisha. At the end of his life, the story implies, Elijah was honoured by God in that he did not die naturally but was taken up into heaven (2 Kings 2:11)—a mark of closeness to God matched by only a few, such as Enoch (Genesis 5:24). Centuries later, when Jesus climbed up a mountain with three of his disciples to be transformed in front of them into something like his eternal 'image', two figures met him there, representing the two great pillars of ancient Israelite history: the Law and the Prophets. One was Moses, who had had an experience of being transfigured on a mountain once before (Exodus 34:29–30). Who was the other? Not Elisha. Not Isaiah, who prophesied the suffering servant, or Jeremiah, who prophesied the new covenant. Not Ezekiel, Daniel or any one of a number of others who might have represented the prophetic ministry of Israel—but Elijah. Demoted? I don't think so.

But if the call to anoint Elisha was not a demotion or a punishment, what was it, and why did it come at this moment? I think it was, in fact, a sign of transition in Elijah's life. I think it was only when Elijah had learnt the crucial difference between calling down fire and listening for the still, small voice that he was ready to train and teach another prophet. Far from being a punishment ('you will be replaced'), this instruction to anoint Elisha is a transition into a new era of maturity in ministry ('now you are ready to be trusted to train a younger prophet').

Perhaps, in addition, giving Elijah an apprentice or team member was exactly what he needed to meet his own weakness. Elijah and Elisha lived at a time when prophets were not usually isolated individuals, but worked together in teams or 'schools'. I work as a college chaplain in the University of Cambridge and, as the only member of the clergy in my institution, there is the potential to become isolated. I have two safeguards. One is staying in touch with other college and university chaplains, but the other is volunteering to supervise an ordinand or minister-in-training. That ordinand or trainee works alongside me for a year, and I give him or her all sorts of opportunities and tasks during the year, meeting up regularly to review the learning process and how his or her understanding of ministry is developing. But all the people to whom I have given a training place have become much more than trainees. They have become team members. I put in the time to supervise their learning but I also learn from them. They come into my 'patch' with a fresh perspective and they often see more clearly than I do where things are working well and where things are a bit tired or clunky. They see what I can't see, so I listen to them. I take on board what they tell me so that I don't become lost in my own ideas of how the world should be. They give me fresh perspective and cheerful company, and they make me laugh. If I was ever in danger of believing that I am the only 'prophet' left in my college, they certainly save me from that delusion!

Perhaps entrusting Elisha into Elijah's care was a mark of God's trust, not his disapproval. I hope so—but I also think it was for the benefit of both. Elisha needed to learn but Elijah also needed his protégé so that he would not be alone. Elisha would help him keep a sense of perspective, keep him young, and stop him getting lost in the traps of workaholism and perfectionism.

[14 December]

The beginning of the end

I will stand at my watchpost, and station myself on the rampart;
I will keep watch to see what he will say to me,
and what he will answer concerning my complaint.
Then the Lord answered me and said:
Write the vision; make it plain on tablets,
so that a runner may read it.
For there is still a vision for the appointed time;
it speaks of the end, and does not lie.
If it seems to tarry, wait for it;
it will surely come, it will not delay...

I hear, and I tremble within; my lips quiver at the sound.
Rottenness enters into my bones, and my steps tremble beneath me.
I wait quietly for the day of calamity
to come upon the people who attack us.
Though the fig tree does not blossom, and no fruit is on the vines;
though the produce of the olive fails and the fields yield no food;
though the flock is cut off from the fold
and there is no herd in the stalls,
yet I will rejoice in the Lord;
I will exult in the God of my salvation.
God, the Lord, is my strength;
he makes my feet like the feet of a deer,
and makes me tread upon the heights.

HABAKKUK 2:1–3; 3:16–19

The main focus of the season of Advent is the anticipation of a new beginning, a new era that would be brought in by the birth of

Christ. Looking back to the first Christmas, we naturally think of the messianic promise as a beginning—the beginning of the era that led to our present existence. But a parallel idea, the anticipation of the second coming of Christ, is also woven into the themes of Advent. This has more in common, perhaps, with the perspective of those who, before the first Christmas, had been waiting through generations for a promised Messiah.

Through many generations of the people of ancient Israel, it was hoped that the Messiah would bring the end of exile, the end of oppression, the end of political occupation, the end of violence and the end of poverty. The idea of the Messiah as an apocalyptic hope had as much to do with a sense of ending as it did with a new beginning. Even Jesus himself spoke in mysterious, apocalyptic terms of the end of the world, or the Day of the Lord (see, for example, Luke 21; Matthew 24). The prophets and Jesus described the signs of the end of the world, including natural disasters and dislocations in the patterns of the stars, the sun and the moon. This has an acutely contemporary resonance. The last few years have seen dramatic natural disasters: floods, tsunami, hurricanes, earthquakes and volcanoes have devastated lives and communities all over the globe. Every day there is something in the news about the state of the earth in relation to the rest of the known universe, and some prediction or other of what may happen to the earth and the human race if particular changes or events take place. So does that mean the end of the world is nigh?

There are countless stories of millennial groups who have expected the end of the world to come imminently. The Catholic Apostolic Church, as legend has it, built their churches on shallow foundations in order that when the rapture came they would be lifted up—people, bricks and all—into the heavens. Other sects have estimated the date of the world's end and stood out in fields, watching the sky, waiting to be taken up into the clouds with Jesus. One by one they have been left looking foolish because, despite their best efforts to read the signs of the times, they got it wrong. The following week they would be found sheepishly doing the washing, going back to work, popping down the shops and working out where their calculations went awry. It's not really that easy to know when the end is coming.

The 'end of the world' as a phrase has much more reality for us when it is taken not literally but metaphorically. There are moments when, on a personal level, we feel that our world really has ended. Most of us experience some kind of trauma at least once or twice in our lives, and when we do, we can't see how life will ever be normal again. Maybe we feel that way after a death, a redundancy or some failure or disappointment; maybe during illness or after an accident; maybe when a relationship breaks down. At those times, our own little world does seem to come to an end. Everything takes on an air of unreality; everything seems frozen in time. Yet the rest of the world goes on exactly the same as usual. 'Why don't they all stop?' we think. 'Why can't they see that nothing will ever be the same again?'

Seeing our lives in terms of endings and beginnings can help to give us a sense of perspective. It can restore a sense of purpose to what might otherwise be just an endless cycle of events. When my son was born, I wrote to a friend whom I don't see very often to tell him the news. I had a long letter back the following week, in which he told me that the same night my son was born, he had been sitting by a bedside in the very same hospital with his father, who was dying. My friend said that he had found it utterly bewildering to have lost a parent, but receiving the news that, within the walls of one hospital, as his world seemed to grind to a halt, mine was just opening up in a new way had a strangely healing effect on him. The pain in the end of one life was somehow eased by the beginning of another. This feeling that the ending of one life was not the end of the whole world, but was giving way to the beginning of another life, somehow gave him the sense of continuity he needed to carry on.

The knowledge that we come from somewhere, and that we have an ultimate purpose, is the very reason we spend Advent thinking about the creation of the world (the great beginning) and the double meaning of the coming of Christ: his first coming at Christmas, the beginning of a new era in human history, and his second coming that symbolizes the end of all things. We need to know that we have a purpose. We come from somewhere, and we are going somewhere.

Habakkuk speaks of the end in terms of absolute catastrophe; there is little hope to alleviate his grim predictions. To the extent that there is hope, it is not a hope for a future life on this earth. Yet he is intriguingly resolute in the meantime. 'Though the fig tree does not blossom, and no fruit is on the vines... yet I will rejoice' (3:17–18). For me, it has been the lesson of recent years not to wait for circumstances to improve before I start to celebrate life. Life is a gift from God, and we do not know how many days we have. Even when times are lean, even in the midst of dark days, even when we see endings coming our way, 'yet I will rejoice...'. If we wait for things to get better before we learn to enjoy and celebrate the days we have, we may waste most of our lives in waiting. Advent is about waiting in one sense, but perhaps the lesson of this season is to live while we wait, to recognize that waiting is simply part of life, not a prelude to it.

'Yet I will rejoice...' could become our prayer, our defiant motto, for every day, come what may. In this, we ourselves become prophetic—not so much through what we say, but in the fact that our daily lives become an emblem of hope and an icon of promise. We can see the end coming, but we are still living in between.

[15 December]

Every valley shall be exalted

Comfort, O comfort my people, says your God.
Speak tenderly to Jerusalem, and cry to her
that she has served her term, that her penalty is paid,
that she has received from the Lord's hand
double for all her sins.

A voice cries out:
'In the wilderness prepare the way of the Lord,
make straight in the desert a highway for our God.
Every valley shall be lifted up,
and every mountain and hill be made low;
the uneven ground shall become level,
and the rough places a plain.
Then the glory of the Lord shall be revealed,
and all people shall see it together,
for the mouth of the Lord has spoken.' ...

Get you up to a high mountain, O Zion, herald of good tidings;
lift up your voice with strength, O Jerusalem, herald of good tidings,
lift it up, do not fear;
say to the cities of Judah, 'Here is your God!'
See, the Lord God comes with might, and his arm rules for him;
his reward is with him, and his recompense before him.
He will feed his flock like a shepherd;
he will gather the lambs in his arms, and carry them in his bosom,
and gently lead the mother sheep.

ISAIAH 40:1–5, 9–11

'The hills will be brought level with the valleys, and the roads made straight, not crooked.' I'm writing this looking out over the flat countryside of the Fens. The deepest valley for miles around is no more than twelve feet deep. The highest hill hardly blocks the view. I was born on the edge of the Peak District, in a house built on a very steep slope, and later moved to a market town in Lincolnshire where the hills were less steep but the countryside was still undulating. So when I first moved to the Fens, I found the countryside very bleak and featureless, and struggled to see beauty in it. One day I was chatting to a native of East Anglia, who remarked on the beautiful view. I must have looked puzzled, failing to see it myself, as my conversation partner looked at me for a moment and said, 'You need to look up. You never see a sky like this in places with hills. Here, there's nothing to block the view.'

Sure enough, I began to adjust my view and learn the profound beauty of the skies of East Anglia. Where every hill is levelled and every valley raised up, there is the possibility for a different kind of revelation, where the light is clear. Artists come here to paint and writers to write because, despite a certain bleakness about the landscape, the light has a clarity that makes you see things in a new way. On one level, I don't think anything will ever cure me of my love for the hills and gorges of the Peak District, but the spiritual lesson is one worth grasping—that where everything can be seen and everything is on a level plane, there is a unique revelation of the lights of the sky.

Isaiah uses a dizzying range and mixture of metaphors for God in this passage. He tells us that God's 'arm rules for him' (v. 10), a military allusion to might and power. But the militarism is balanced in the same verse with a picture of justice ('his reward is with him, and his recompense before him') and then adjusted to one of extreme pastoral intimacy—of feeding, gathering and carrying his flock in his arms, or 'in his bosom' (v. 11). This suggests the closest and most tender carrying, often associated with a mother but equally possible for any caring adult. So we see might, power, justice, tenderness and intimacy all rolled together. Often, Christian interpretations of the prophets will major on one or other of these kinds of images, with the result that God is over-interpreted one way or another. The God represented by some churches is so strong and powerful, so extreme in standing up for moral justice, that the justice delivered lacks any kind of mercy or compassion. Tough love can be too tough—but equally, a God who is all feathersoft can be one who is so compassionate that there cannot be any justice.

True justice requires both toughness against wrongdoing, and infinite care and compassion for the victim. This is a complex mixture for any person or any group to achieve, especially when we consider that the perpetrators of injustice are sometimes victims in their own right. Often, the only adequate pastoral care will require both extreme toughness and endless compassion. I am glad that the prophets call us to hold this complex and complete picture as our image of God. We may fail to live up to it ourselves, but the trouble really begins if we lose sight of the fact that God holds these qualities of love, wisdom, power and justice in perfect proportion.

Meantime, the comfort that Isaiah announces is not feathersoft either. 'Comfort' has a narrower range of meaning now than it did at one time. When the King James Bible was translated, to comfort meant to encourage, not just by soothing but by giving a swift jab in the ribs. 'Comfort my people' might include wrapping them up and soothing them—certainly if we take the image of the shepherd seriously—but it also means the kind of pep talk that we would get from a coach who stands on the sidelines and shouts to make us run faster, keep going, not give up.

So Isaiah gives us a God who brings comfort, but comfort in the sense of encouragement that will feel as much like a sharp dig in the ribs as the softness of a warm duvet. This is a God of power, but in the sense of devolving power out to the powerless, levelling up the scales of justice. This is a God who carries out the pastoral care of gathering, feeding and carrying with great tenderness—a mother as much as a father; a shepherd as much as a warrior; a mentor and a friend.

The wilderness is an idea that the biblical writers return to over and over again. David lived there while he was fighting with King Saul. Elijah ran there to escape from Jezebel. John lived there, eating locusts and honey. Jesus went there after his baptism and experienced his temptations there. The wilderness is a place of extremes, a place of difficult physical circumstances yet great spiritual illumination. If you go today to the areas these stories describe, you will find vast tracts of land where there is little but sand and rocks, not much water and not a great deal of vegetation.

In European religious art of the 16th and 17th centuries, we can often see the wilderness depicted as a forest, which sounds lush compared to a sandy desert but, for the artists of the time, is exactly what the idea of wilderness summoned up. Just as Middle European fairytales often depict the forest as a place of danger and menace, where people get lost and never return, so the religious artists imagined the wilderness as a deep, dark and dangerous forest.

'A voice cries out, "In the wilderness prepare the way of the Lord"' (v. 3). Sometimes this verses is translated rather differently: 'A voice cries out in the wilderness, "Prepare the way of the Lord"' (see KJV). What is Isaiah suggesting here? Is it that the voice that is announcing the Lord is to be found in the wilderness? Or is it that the voice calls us to go to the wilderness to prepare? There is no punctuation in the original biblical text to help us here, but maybe, in fact, both are equally true. On the one hand, the voice that announced Jesus was the voice of John, who did live out in the desert, and, on the other hand, Jesus himself went out into the wilderness to prepare himself for ministry. Maybe, like Elijah (see readings for 11–13 December), it's only when we move out of our daily routine that we become still enough to hear God's voice. Or maybe there is something about a place of danger and threat that sharpens our senses.

All in one short passage, then, Isaiah gives us a multifaceted image of God who comes to us with comfort and bracing encouragement, justice and revelation. The question is, are we prepared to face the wilderness in order to find it?

[16 December]

Gaudete Sunday: already and not yet

There was a man sent from God, whose name was John. He came as a witness to testify to the light, so that all might believe through him. He himself was not the light, but he came to testify to the light…

This is the testimony given by John when the Jews sent priests and Levites from Jerusalem to ask him, 'Who are you?' He confessed and did not deny it, but confessed, 'I am not the Messiah.' And they asked him, 'What then? Are you Elijah?' He said, 'I am not.' 'Are you the prophet?' He answered, 'No.' Then they said to him, 'Who are you? Let us have an answer for those who sent us. What do you say about yourself?' He said, 'I am the voice of one crying out in the wilderness, "Make straight the way of the Lord"', as the prophet Isaiah said. Now they had been sent from the Pharisees. They asked him, 'Why then are you baptizing if you are neither the Messiah, nor Elijah, nor the prophet?' John answered them, 'I baptize with water. Among you stands one whom you do not know, the one who is coming after me; I am not worthy to untie the thong of his sandal.' This took place in Bethany across the Jordan where John was baptizing.

JOHN 1:6–8, 19–28

Keeping Advent goes back at least as far as the fifth century, and it was originally a 40-day fast in preparation for Christmas, beginning the day after St Martin's day (12 November). Advent was shortened to four weeks in the ninth century, and by the twelfth century the fast had been replaced by simple abstinence. It has changed in some ways, then, but it has consistently remained a penitential season—like Lent, a time for waiting on God and for purification.

In contemporary terms, we might describe it as a time for self-assessment and, with the help of God and of those we trust to give us spiritual guidance, a time to bring our lives into better order.

The third Sunday of Advent, also known as Gaudete Sunday, is traditionally a day for breaking the fast. The name comes from the Introit (opening) of the Mass for that day: *Gaudete in Domine Semper*, 'Rejoice in the Lord always'. Back when the Advent fast was kept strictly, flowers and musical instruments were forbidden in church during Advent and Lent, and clergy were always robed in purple or black. But on the middle Sunday of Advent, music and flowers were permitted, and priests and deacons would wear rose-coloured vestments instead, to mark this day of relief in the middle of the fast. This is why, if you use a purple set of Advent candles, you'll find that the third one is pink instead of purple. Gaudete Sunday is a reminder that Advent is passing swiftly, and that the Lord's coming is near. The focus turns more to the second coming than the first, thus heightening the sense of intense joy, gladness and expectation. For one day, the spirit of penitence in preparation for Christmas and the coming Messiah is suspended in favour of a joyful anticipation of the promised redemption—the 'already-but-not-yet' idea that permeates the entire mindset of the Christian believer. The Gospel readings for Gaudete Sunday always revolve around the story of John the Baptist, and the third Advent Candle is lit in honour of him.

The whole thrust of John's ministry is the announcement that the Lord's coming is near—in fact, nearer than you think. The people who went to listen to John in the desert were longing for political freedom, and their hopes rested on the promised Messiah. What could a Messiah be like? A strong and powerful person, a charismatic leader, a political firebrand? And where would he come from? There's one thing you can practically guarantee if you are looking for a striking and impressive leader: it won't be someone from your own community. Why? Because it's so much easier to believe in someone when all we see is their strengths, their good points, their potential. It's much harder to believe in someone if we've seen them fall down in the playground, fail an exam or be dumped by a girlfriend or two. Once we've seen someone in all their humanity, it's much harder to believe in them as a superhero.

'Among you stands one whom you do not know,' says John (v. 26). What you are hoping for, waiting for, expecting, anticipating (John says to the downtrodden people)—it's already here! But you can't see it. He is on the verge of making himself known. The 'already-but-not-yet' of the kingdom is perfectly summed up in this story. The person they were hoping for was on their doorstep. Christ himself was living right there among them, yet they didn't recognize him. I guess, if you're waiting for a superhero, you might not notice the saint quietly growing up in the builder's yard at Nazareth.

Perhaps for us, too, the hope we invest in Jesus can sometimes take a shape in our minds that stops us from noticing his presence. Maybe God is with us and we haven't noticed; maybe we don't recognize him because we have a fixed idea in our minds of what he will look like when he appears.

Interestingly, though, even Jesus himself seems to have needed John's ministry to bring him out from a 'not yet' frame of mind and catalyse his ministry. There are several places where John, by his words or actions, opens up the next chapter for Jesus. Here, it is John who singles him out in the crowd and identifies him as God's chosen one.

Why Jesus needed John to confirm his identity and calling is not entirely clear. It wasn't clear to John either, who was somewhat dumbfounded at the idea that he should baptize Jesus. Perhaps Jesus' own sense of identity was not fully formed within him until John clarified it for him. We will never know quite how and when Jesus grew to understand his unique identity and calling, but the story of John identifying Jesus and calling him out from the crowd gives us food for thought about our own identity and calling.

The convergence of personal offering and objective recognition is essential to our calling. When I began to consider offering myself for ordination, I was concerned that I had no clear evidence to say that I 'knew' God had called me. A wise priest, much older than me, told me then that calling is rarely accompanied by a dramatic, personal epiphany on the lines of a Damascus Road experience. Much more often, for the individual concerned, the realization that a certain set of gifts and inclinations are leading in a particular direction has to be combined with the willingness to accept the idea of a vocation. But in addition, it isn't the sole responsibility of the individual to discern her or his calling. In the case of a calling into ministry or another form of holy orders, it is not just that God calls the individual privately, but that the Church also calls her priests. There is no such thing, in true church theology, as a private 'calling'.

Ordination, of course, is only one kind of calling. Every person is called, by God and by the Church, to discover and fulfil their place in the world. When that calling is not specifically religious in nature, it's easy to overlook the fact that we are called (or should be!) by the Church as well as by God, and that we discover our calling less often through a personal epiphany than through a gradual recognition of gifts and inclinations, coupled with a willingness to become whatever God wants us to be.

Our callings are not limited merely to jobs with religious identities. Our calling as Christians is to find our place in the world so that all our gifts—all that we are, and all that we have—can be fulfilled in such a way that God is glorified and the world is served. Again, words like 'ordination' are so religious in their connotations that we can miss the vitality of their meaning. A calling isn't meant to make us more sober, more 'religious', more worthy, but to bring us joy and enable us to become more fully human. As the second-century theologian Irenaeus said, 'The glory of God is man fully alive.'

This little vignette of the two cousins, John and Jesus, shows that even the Son of God relied upon someone who was both a relative and a religious leader to confirm his calling. How much more, then, do we need each other in the Church to identify each other's callings?

[SECTION 4]

Angels and announcements: How does God speak to us, and how do we hear?

In this section I want to look at some accounts in which people heard an announcement from God, either in an encounter with the Lord or through an angelic messenger sent from God. There are certain similarities between these stories—the idea that God is magnificent and impressive, the idea that angels always start their messages with the words 'Fear not'—and there are patterns that follow: people are uncomfortable and need reassurance of one kind or another to be able to accept the message from God. But there are also striking differences between the accounts. Those who receive God's message might be thoughtful and deliberate, carefree and blithely accepting, cynical and unbelieving, or overwhelmed with self-doubt.

From these extraordinary accounts in which God announces the beginnings of new things, we might glean some wisdom as to how we hear and how we react to the voice of God.

[17 December]

Unclean lips and the problem of language

In the year that King Uzziah died, I saw the Lord sitting on a throne, high and lofty; and the hem of his robe filled the temple. Seraphs were in attendance above him; each had six wings: with two they covered their faces, and with two they covered their feet, and with two they flew. And one called to another and said: 'Holy, holy, holy is the Lord of hosts; the whole earth is full of his glory.' The pivots on the thresholds shook at the voices of those who called, and the house filled with smoke. And I said: 'Woe is me! I am lost, for I am a man of unclean lips, and I live among a people of unclean lips; yet my eyes have seen the King, the Lord of hosts!' Then one of the seraphs flew to me, holding a live coal that had been taken from the altar with a pair of tongs. The seraph touched my mouth with it and said: 'Now that this has touched your lips, your guilt has departed and your sin is blotted out.' Then I heard the voice of the Lord saying, 'Whom shall I send, and who will go for us?' And I said, 'Here am I; send me!'

ISAIAH 6:1–8

The Bible is often thought of as a single book, whereas in fact it is a collection of widely different pieces of writing, from different eras and in different literary forms. It is also often treated not as a collection of different kinds of literature, but as a kind of instruction manual for Christian living. Such expectations of the Bible are fraught with difficulties. The Bible was written, rewritten, edited and translated by different people from different times and different cultures, so it's not surprising that it refuses to provide the degree of uniformity and consistency that we would expect from a single book by a single author. If we looked at a 20th-century chemistry textbook, a 19th-century newspaper, a TV instruction manual badly translated from Japanese into English, an election flyer and a Jane Austen novel, our picture of English life would be partly accurate, but it would be an incomplete patchwork of images. It's the same, only more so, with the Bible. Treating the Bible purely as a collection of books, we can hardly expect a uniform view of God or of humanity to emerge from its pages.

Part of our problem in reading and making sense of the Bible comes from the mostly unspoken belief that if it is God's word to us, surely it must be clear, consistent and dependable. Yet when we actually read it, we find that the Bible sometimes tells us things we don't want to know about, and doesn't tell us what we do want to know. We find that it has awkward contradictions, and obscure bits that we don't know what to do with, and it leaps all over the place in style and subject matter. It seems that we have to either find complex methods of rationalizing away the difficulties and inconsistencies, or admit that it's a difficult book to make sense of and doesn't 'work' as a simple manual of Christian living. And if we do that, will it still be God's word to us?

Perhaps, though, a steady consistency is not necessary in order to hear what the Bible has to tell us about God and human relationships. Perhaps it is precisely the variety and inconsistency of these accounts that enable us to separate the central threads in the narrative through the passage of time and the shifts in culture. Perhaps it is only when we take account of the limitations of human language and the variety of human experience that we are able to hear God's voice. We need to have our feet on the ground, even when our hearts are searching the heavens.

Isaiah's call opens up this problem of language and communication. Isaiah saw the Lord, seated on a great throne in the temple and surrounded by angels. The angels reacted to the presence of God by calling out to each other their adoration of him. How beautiful God's appearance must have been, how overwhelming his presence, how completely absorbing the sense of his goodness and love, to draw this constant stream of adoration! Even the temple building itself reacted to God's presence, shaking at its foundations and filling with smoke.

The temple had been built, so it was believed, according to God's own specifications, and was entirely devoted to the worship of God. If there was anywhere that could take the presence of God, this was the place. But when God himself actually appeared, the building shook. Plenty of other characters in the Bible are recorded as falling down in worship, like these seraphs, or shaking with fear, or even falling down in a dead faint when faced with God's presence. Yet while the building shook and the angels worshipped, Isaiah himself seems to have stayed on his feet. It was the temple, not the man, that was physically overcome.

Isaiah, though, was overcome with the stark revelation that he—a holy man who was admitted to the holiest parts of the temple—seemed, in the presence of God, to be entirely inadequate. His sense of sinfulness and unworthiness was very specific; it was not that he had a guilty conscience about his actions. Isaiah, it seems, was someone who lived up to the expectations of a priest—his life was commendable and good—but standing in the presence of the Lord, hearing the voices of the angels, he felt suddenly that his voice was a clanging bell. Like a pub singer, perhaps, in the presence of a great diva, or a street preacher in the presence of a great orator, Isaiah suddenly felt small, cheap and worthless by comparison to what he saw in front of him. It wasn't that he felt he should be a better person. It was that the presence of God so far surpassed what it was to be human that he felt himself laid completely bare. His lips, he said, were unclean. All his words were ashes. He had nothing to say.

It's one of the frustrations of human language that it is the only and best tool of communication that we have at our disposal, and yet it is insufficient in its capacity to communicate what we want to say. As the French novelist Gustave Flaubert put it in *Madame Bovary*, 'Human language is like a cracked pot on which we beat out our rhythms for bears to dance to, when we are striving to make music that will wring tears from stars.'

Every poet, every songwriter, every preacher, every lover, has surely run up against this sense of empty inadequacy in language: the words said out loud never seem quite to match the intent of the imagination. Life itself is dogged sometimes with the same impossibility. We may set out to live with hope and imagination, vigour and enthusiasm, yet at times we turn to look at our own lives and they seem as empty as clothes hanging in a wardrobe. Geoffrey Studdert Kennedy compared life to language in his poem 'It is not finished':

I cannot read the writing of the years,
My eyes are full of tears,
It gets all blurred and won't make sense
It's full of contradictions
Like the scribblings of a child.

I can but hand it in, and hope
That Thy great mind, which reads
The writings of so many lives,
Will understand this scrawl
And what it strives
To say—but leaves unsaid.

God appoints messengers, those who will say what needs to be heard. Sometimes the messengers are angels, and sometimes—like Isaiah, or the countless other individuals who spoke and wrote the words that were eventually collected into the Bible—they are people. Those people find that both their lives and their words are inadequate to articulate the vision and the hope that they have grasped in their glimpses of the presence of God. The question, though, seems to be less to do with whether they are good communicators than whether they are realistic about their abilities and willing to be faithful to the task, at least as far as their abilities allow. Humility and faithfulness do not eliminate imperfection, but they are essential if the messenger is to be effective. A messenger has to be self-effacing enough for the message to come through; messengers who are too full of themselves obscure the view.

We can allow, then, for imperfection in the words of scripture without thinking that it eliminates God's message. The wonder of life and the glory of God can still be communicated through the imperfect means of human lives and human language. In fact, simply owning up to the fact that the Bible is only as good a means of communication as human language can ever be frees the Bible to be a text that 'speaks' to us.

Having said that, we might still, despite the limitations of language, take hope from Isaiah's commission from God. It was, perhaps, precisely his own recognition that within himself he had nothing to say that qualified him to become God's mouthpiece. It's worth noticing that the action of the seraph in touching Isaiah's lips was not to improve his capacity with language, or to make him speak better words, but to cleanse his sin. Our human abilities don't need to be bypassed in order for God to be revealed through our words and our lives. Rather, it is when we recognize and accept the limitations of human language that the 'something more' that is God can shine through. It was God's choice, both then and now, to speak through the cracked and broken vessels of human language and human lives, not superseding human life but working with people who had enough humility simply to be human.

[18 December]

Zechariah: the man who had waited too long

In the days of King Herod of Judea, there was a priest named Zechariah, who belonged to the priestly order of Abijah. His wife was a descendant of Aaron, and her name was Elizabeth. Both of them were righteous before God, living blamelessly according to all the commandments and regulations of the Lord. But they had no children, because Elizabeth was barren, and both were getting on in years.

Once when he was serving as priest before God and his section was on duty, he was chosen by lot, according to the custom of the priesthood, to enter the sanctuary of the Lord and offer incense. Now at the time of the incense-offering, the whole assembly of the people was praying outside. Then there appeared to him an angel of the Lord, standing at the right side of the altar of incense. When Zechariah saw him, he was terrified; and fear overwhelmed him. But the angel said to him, 'Do not be afraid, Zechariah, for your prayer has been heard. Your wife Elizabeth will bear you a son, and you will name him John. You will have joy and gladness, and many will rejoice at his birth, for he will be great in the sight of the Lord. He must never drink wine or strong drink; even before his birth he will be filled with the Holy Spirit. He will turn many of the people of Israel to the Lord their God. With the spirit and power of Elijah he will go before him, to turn the hearts of parents to their children, and the disobedient to the wisdom of the righteous, to make ready a people prepared for the Lord.' Zechariah said to the angel, 'How will I know that this is so? For I am an old man, and my wife is getting on in years.' The angel replied, 'I am Gabriel. I stand in the presence of God, and I have been sent to speak to you and to bring you this good news. But now, because you did not believe my words, which will be fulfilled in their time, you will become mute, unable to speak, until the day these things occur.'

LUKE 1:5–20

When something has been hoped for, longed for, expected over a very long time, sometimes the actual expectation loses touch with reality. It is as if the hope has been held so long that the heart has gone out of it, or that the repeated deferral of hope has replaced expectation with a sense of impossibility. People who have lived alone with the wish to be married, people who have lived childless for many years while longing for a baby, people who have lived with chronic illness in the hope of a cure, or people who have worked on a project or a cause for years and never quite seen it come to fruition—all of these, in a way, have never given up hope, yet they have grown used to living with the constant failure of the hope to become a reality. It's as if the heart goes a little cold, anaesthetizing itself against more disappointment.

For someone in that position, when the longed-for outcome suddenly becomes a genuine possibility, it seems completely unbelievable. In our world of IVF treatments, we are familiar with stories of parents who have waited year upon year for a baby that never materializes, only to find it amazing and beyond belief when they finally find that they are expecting a child. How much more unbelievable it must have been for Zechariah and Elizabeth, whose hope of a baby had faded almost to nothing.

Zechariah's capacity for hope had been dimmed to the point that even when an angel stood before him he couldn't believe the words he was hearing. It wasn't that he couldn't be sure it was an angel. Most of the time, when we are trying to discern a way forward, all we have to go on is an inner voice, our conscience, our accrued wisdom, or the counsel of others. It is only sane and responsible to question such voices and weigh them up in the process of decision making. But Zechariah was evidently not listening to an inner voice. His encounter with the angel was tangible and grand enough to make him terrified, overwhelmed by fear, and yet, despite the reality of the vision, he still doubted the words he heard. It's tempting to assume that such a clear mandate from God would be easy to take on board. How often we wish we could have, in the place of tough decision making, some clear indication of a 'right' way forward, a way of knowing that the decision we make is guided by God's wisdom. Yet Zechariah's experience suggests that, if we are in a particular frame of mind, even the Archangel Gabriel himself is not enough to convince the unbelieving mind as to God's counsel.

What is it that makes one person completely, unshakeably confident in a soft inner voice, and another unable to believe even when an angel visits them? What stopped Zechariah from believing his own eyes and ears when such a clear message was delivered to him? Perhaps he just couldn't bear the idea of going through the cycle of hope and disappointment one more time. Perhaps he had just grown so cynical that even the appearance of an angel failed to impress him. We'll never know, but what we do know is that Zechariah could not believe what he heard, and demanded some kind of proof or guarantee from God—some means of assurance that what he had seen and heard was real and not just his imagination or a trick of the light.

Taking the story as simple human reportage, it seems a bit unfair on poor old Zechariah. Most accounts of a call from God allow for the recipient to be somewhat flabbergasted. Moses, Jeremiah, Abraham, Job, Peter, even Mary the mother of Jesus—all these were allowed their moment of questioning as they struggled to take in God's message. Most of them even had their questions answered. What was so different about Zechariah's response?

There is a striking similarity between the setting of Zechariah's story and the call of Isaiah that we read yesterday. Amid the smoky incense, each of them saw some glorious vision of heaven and heard the message of God. There's a link between their reactions, too, though in the mode of a reversal—taking an expected idea and turning it upside down, or reversing the dynamic of a traditional story to make a point. Reversal is a literary device used a lot in the biblical birth narratives, and this is a good example. The similarity between Isaiah 6 and Luke 1 is unavoidable, but the point at which the story moves in the opposite direction places the spotlight for us and gives us a broad hint as to what the main point of the story is.

Isaiah said, 'Woe is me, for I am a man of unclean lips' (6:5). Like Moses before him, Isaiah doubted his own capacity to be God's mouthpiece. Zechariah seems not to be questioning his own capacity or worthiness; nor does he seem to be puzzling out how the events will occur. Rather, he seems to be questioning the veracity of the message itself—questioning how trustworthy the Lord's words actually are. 'Prove it to me,' he seems to be saying; 'show me a sign.' So, in a reversal of the parallel story of Isaiah, the sign he is given is the antithesis of the Isaiah story: instead of becoming God's mouthpiece, as Isaiah did, he becomes unable to speak at all. God is sending an important message and is choosing a messenger to be the herald of the good news. Isaiah's lips were touched and purified; Zechariah's lips were sealed. The point of the story is that God will speak, and God will choose his messenger.

Zechariah's muteness, then, is not a punishment for his unbelief but a response to his own request for a sign. The sign God gave him, a temporary inability to speak, was symbolically linked to the angel's message in two ways. First of all, falling silent as he did in the temple, Zechariah would have been unable to pronounce the priestly blessing at the end of his duties. Raymond E. Brown makes the connection between this and the priestly ministry of Jesus, pointing to the fact that at the end of Luke's Gospel, it was Jesus himself who gave a priestly blessing (24:50–52). In addition, I think there is significance to Zechariah's silence in that, as the father of John the herald, he himself is silenced. His son will proclaim the coming kingdom, and (in a nice touch which is typical of Luke, who everywhere includes the place of women in his Gospel) it is Elizabeth and not Zechariah who gets to broadcast the good news (1:42–45). So the priestly ministry of the temple was symbolically silenced to make way for the emergence of John, who would be the herald of the new covenant, and Jesus, who would be the great high priest.

Now, I'll grant you that symbolic value wouldn't have made it any more fun for Zechariah to be unable to utter a word for the best part of a year—but speaking is key to the ministry of John the Baptist. John was going to proclaim the coming Messiah and eventually confirm and catalyse the ministry of Jesus by speaking prophetic words—words that inspire faith. In preparation for this prophetic task, the words of unbelief were silenced.

[19 December]

Don't hurry: perplexed and pondering

In the sixth month the angel Gabriel was sent by God to a town in Galilee called Nazareth, to a virgin engaged to a man whose name was Joseph, of the house of David. The virgin's name was Mary. And he came to her and said, 'Greetings, favoured one! The Lord is with you.' But she was much perplexed by his words and pondered what sort of greeting this might be. The angel said to her, 'Do not be afraid, Mary, for you have found favour with God. And now, you will conceive in your womb and bear a son, and you will name him Jesus. He will be great, and will be called the Son of the Most High, and the Lord God will give to him the throne of his ancestor David. He will reign over the house of Jacob for ever, and of his kingdom there will be no end.'

LUKE 1:26–33

What must it be like to meet an archangel? There are stories throughout the scriptures, and in popular religious literature, of people who have encountered angels, or the Lord in human form, or both together. There is remarkable variety in the reports of their experience.

In some accounts, the experience is so mundane that they don't initially recognize that they are seeing God. For instance, when Abraham was visited by three men in his desert home, he welcomed them as all strangers would be welcomed (Genesis 18). Recently I met a woman from Inner Mongolia, one of the few places where nomadic lifestyles are still common. She told me that in her culture, both in nomadic and urban communities, it is simply taken as read that strangers who come across your path are offered all the basic necessities of life. The extreme climate means that automatic hospitality can be the difference between life and death, and it is assumed that the hospitality you offer to someone in need may be repaid to you by someone else at a later date. Abraham was following just this kind of convention. He was not giving these strangers special treatment; he was treating them in the way anyone in a nomadic culture would be treated. It isn't entirely clear at what stage in the story he realized that these were no ordinary human beings. By the time he had walked with his mysterious guests towards Sodom, though, he definitely knew who he was talking to. He may have been awe-inspired, but he continued to cook their meal, walk and talk with them and even argue with the Lord himself, after the two angels walked on ahead (vv. 22–33).

Biblical characters have had various reactions to receiving messages directly from God or from angelic figures. Moses was so physically affected by his brush with God's presence that his face shone with God's glory (Exodus 34:29). As we have seen, when Isaiah encountered the Lord, the temple shook at its foundations while he himself, although amazed, stayed on his feet and continued a conversation with God (Isaiah 6). When Ezekiel saw the glory of God, he fell face down (Ezekiel 1:28), and centuries later, on the island of Patmos, when John encountered the Lord in human form he fell completely unconscious and had to be revived (Revelation 1:17).

We read here in Luke's Gospel that when Mary was visited by Gabriel, she was at first 'perplexed' (v. 29)—not quite as strong a reaction as Zechariah's terror (v. 12), but pretty shaken up all the same. The angel then said, 'Don't be afraid'—words which are spoken so often by angels that we might reasonably construe that an angelic visitation can be a very fearful and disturbing experience.

We're also told, though, that Mary 'pondered' what kind of message she was being given (v. 29). The word 'ponder' comes from Middle English (also from Middle French and Latin). In England, the word dates back to about 1330, and it meant to measure the weight of something or to estimate its worth. The word 'pound' as a measure of weight comes from the same root. But by 1380 it had taken on more the sense of weighing something up mentally, or of taking some time to consider, rather than making a rushed decision. It seems, then, that Mary had time to pause and reflect during her conversation with the angel.

It is pleasing to think that an angelic visitation is not strictly timed, and that an angel might allow Mary the opportunity to think before giving her the next part of the message. Hi-tech communications increasingly give us the sense that a 'message' is something brief, precise and instant, delivered in a moment and demanding a swift response, but angelic visitors, it seems, are in no such hurry. There is time for silent spaces between conversation. There is no hint here of the pressure of a premium-rate phone call or the anxiety of the next task. Like the unhurried conversation of lovers, there is time for pauses, time to enjoy the presence of the other, time to gaze a little.

This idea of encounter and intimacy is drawn out by Edwin Muir in his poem 'The angel and the girl are met'. The angel comes 'From far beyond the farthest star, Feathered through time...', and the ordinary events and sounds of life clatter on as usual. Yet somewhere in the midst of it all, as if in another dimension altogether, the girl and the angel meet in an extraordinary, timeless encounter between heaven and earth:

But through the endless afternoon
These neither speak nor movement make.
But stare into their deepening trance
As if their grace would never break.

The message from God, then, is not merely a delivery of information. It's a meeting of persons. The important lesson to draw from Mary's story is that the significance of a visitation is not in the angel himself, nor even the message that he bears, but that a connection is made between a person and God. Perhaps we, too, as we pursue our understanding of God, might allow ourselves to expect something more than getting our prayers heard or our questions answered. Perhaps we, too, in conversation with God, might expect not merely to receive information from or about him, but in some sense that we might 'meet' God in an encounter that profoundly changes us deep inside. But if we are to do so, perhaps we, too, need to find the spaces for silence in between conversation.

[20 December]

Questioning God

Mary said to the angel, 'How can this be, since I am a virgin?' The angel said to her, 'The Holy Spirit will come upon you, and the power of the Most High will overshadow you; therefore the child to be born will be holy; he will be called Son of God. And now, your relative Elizabeth in her old age has also conceived a son; and this is the sixth month for her who was said to be barren. For nothing will be impossible with God.' Then Mary said, 'Here am I, the servant of the Lord; let it be with me according to your word.' Then the angel departed from her.

LUKE 1:34–38

Yesterday we noted that Mary's encounter with the angel includes a sense of time elapsing—that the message was not delivered in a hurry but that Mary had time to ponder. Today we see that she also had permission to question. This is doubly interesting, after the rather stern sign that Zechariah received when he dared to question. As we noted on 18 December, there was an element of unbelief about Zechariah's question, a suggestion that he doubted the veracity of God's words. Mary, though, seems to be questioning how events will unfold, not whether they will happen at all. The difference between her 'How will it happen?' and Zechariah's 'How can I be sure?' seems to be only in the intention of the words. Mary, beginning to believe, willing to believe but puzzled and questioning, can ask God questions and get answers. Zechariah questioned God in a more unbending way, as if to say, 'You'll have to convince me first.'

All the same, Mary's response was far from an immediate and subservient acquiescence. A lucid conversation unfolded between her and the angel, with Mary having time to think and permission to question. She was not so dumbstruck that she was unable to consider what the angel was telling her. Mary's response ('Let it be to me...', v. 38) is often quoted, without noting this extended conversation in which she asks questions. Nearly all the great figures of the Bible were, at the moment of their calling, found to be questioning God. Abraham, Sarah, Jacob, Joseph, Moses, David, Jeremiah, Job... it is hard to find anyone who obeyed instantly, silently and meekly, and Mary is no exception. Even this meek and thoughtful girl had questions. Questioning God is an essential part of faith. Jonathan Sacks, the Chief Rabbi of Britain and the Commonwealth, says, 'To be without questions is not a sign of faith, but of lack of depth.' We ask questions, Sacks says, 'not because we doubt, but because we believe'.[2]

Faith allows us to ask questions—but there is a fine line between making the kind of demands that indicate that we are in charge (and not God) and asking the kind of questions that seek to understand who is the God behind the call.

Between the lines of this story, though, is also woven the intriguing idea of a call being a genuine choice. God calls Mary to be the mother of God; he doesn't insist that she will be or impose his will upon her. He waits for her acquiescence. Some have wondered before now whether God had made this call to other 'Marys', who had not been willing to grasp the possibility. There is almost the sense that while Mary ponders and questions and considers, heaven waits with bated breath to see whether this time the offer will be received. What kind of God is willing to allow for the unfolding of salvation to hinge on the decision of a teenage girl in a rural backwater? At the creation, God worked with nothing to create something (Genesis 1:1–2), but this new creation was worked in partnership with humans, and God's plan unfolded only with Mary's cooperation. The call of God is an invitation, not an imposition.

[21 December]

On the margins

In that region there were shepherds living in the fields, keeping watch over their flock by night. Then an angel of the Lord stood before them, and the glory of the Lord shone around them, and they were terrified. But the angel said to them, 'Do not be afraid; for see—I am bringing you good news of great joy for all the people: to you is born this day in the city of David a Saviour, who is the Messiah, the Lord. This will be a sign for you: you will find a child wrapped in bands of cloth and lying in a manger.' And suddenly there was with the angel a multitude of the heavenly host, praising God and saying, 'Glory to God in the highest heaven, and on earth peace among those whom he favours!'

LUKE 2:8–14

Throughout his Gospel, Luke has a bias towards presenting the message of Jesus as the good news for everyone—the gospel for Gentiles as well as Jews, the gospel that includes women and children, the gospel for the poor and the dispossessed, not only for the rich, the educated, the privileged, the 'insiders'. So it's no surprise that the way Luke tells the story, the first people to get the news are shepherds.

It is obvious that shepherds were not rich and privileged people. The shepherds, though, were even more on the margins of society than other ordinary working people. Christmas cards and nativity scenes portray them as benevolent, gentle, pastoral figures but, in fact, those who were paid to stay out in the fields with the sheep were often, in the culture of the time, considered to be rogues and misfits who lived on the edge of society. They were not criminals, necessarily, but they lived on the margins, and they were certainly not desirable company.

There were two groups of outsiders in the town where I grew up. Every Saturday of the year, a group of bikers used to roar into town, park their huge black motorbikes in the main street and stroll about in black leather and big sunglasses. No doubt they wanted to be impressive, but they were perceived as somewhat menacing, so people avoided them. They didn't fit the mould and therefore seemed threatening.

Then, every spring, a group of travellers came to the town for a whole week, with a large funfair. The fairground rides and stalls were erected all the way through the middle of town, and the travellers parked their caravans on the local meadow. In a small market town short of regular entertainment, everyone went to the fair. People were fascinated by the alternative life of these travelling people. How did they live? Where did they go to school? What could it be like to live on the road, with a caravan as your home? Like the bikers, though, they too were treated with suspicion and mistrust and ended up on the edge of society. Outsiders may be benevolent or criminal, kind or hostile, honest or duplicitous. Sometimes they become hostile precisely because they are treated with suspicion. Sometimes they simply keep themselves to themselves and get on with their innocent lives. Sometimes people live outside mainstream society by choice, preferring to keep their distance from it all. But it's rare for an outsider to break through the social barriers from one group to another and become an 'insider', unless he or she is prepared to change to become like the mainstream group.

The shepherds were outsiders. They may have been honest, but they were not trusted. They may have been kind, but they were treated with a degree of fear, simply because they lived outside the accepted social boundaries. Of all the people in Bethlehem, then, why was it this group of outsiders who heard the angels singing? Was it that the angels only appeared to the shepherds? Or was it that the sky was full of the heavenly host all along, for everyone to see, but most of the people were somehow deaf and blind to the sight and sound? A lovely visual image of this idea of the invisible presence of God is seen in *Wings of Desire*, a film by Wim Wenders, in which characters go about their everyday lives completely unaware that angels—visible to the viewer but not to the characters inside the story—are watching over them to comfort and protect them. There are several stories in the Bible that suggest in a similar way that the presence of angels, or even the Lord himself, can go unnoticed or unrecognized. John 20:14 records that Mary Magdalene, outside the empty tomb, was so wrapped up in her own grief that when she encountered the risen Jesus she didn't recognize him, but thought she was talking to a stranger. John the Baptist announced the coming Messiah not as someone about to arrive from far away, but someone standing right there in the crowd, unnoticed and unrecognized. It seems that the kingdom of God is among us and around us all the time, and often we simply do not see it.

There is also a wonderful story in 2 Kings 6, which tells how the prophet Elisha was confronted by a hostile enemy who intended to capture him. Early in the morning, Elisha's servant got up and saw immediately that their city was under siege by horses and chariots and a great army. The servant, understandably, panicked and ran to Elisha, who, serene and untroubled, said, 'Do not be afraid, for there are more with us than there are with them' (v. 16). What was it that Elisha could see, that the servant could not? Elisha prayed for God to open the servant's eyes to see his true situation, and then he saw that 'the mountain was full of horses and chariots of fire all around Elisha' (v. 17).

Here in Luke, once the shepherds heard and believed the announcement of the angel of the Lord, they immediately saw that the sky was full of angels, singing and praising God. The skies over Bethelehem were full of the hosts of heaven, yet the only people who had the time, vision or imagination to take it in were these marginalized, uneducated outsiders.

If we were to restage the Christmas story in the present, who would see the sky filled with angels? Travellers, maybe? Leather-clad bikers? Homeless people sleeping in doorways, teenagers whose insecurity seems to project an air of hostility, the mentally ill, ex-criminals struggling to rehabilitate themselves? All of these groups tend to be isolated and treated with suspicion and fear, and therefore become outsiders in some sense. The question we might ask ourselves, then, is not what was so special about the shepherds, but what it is about society that renders those of us who are 'insiders' incapable of seeing and hearing God when he speaks.

[SECTION 5]

The Holy Family: the timeless in the everyday

We have a huge cultural emphasis on the feast of Christmas, which stems as much from its origins as a midwinter festival as it does from its Christian meaning. Christmas also gains a feeling of being the culmination of events because it falls at the end of our calendar year. In the Church year, though, Christmas is neither the beginning nor the end. In terms of Christian theology, although it's a moment of huge significance, the incarnation is a hinge moment, not an ending. It is the time that brings long years of waiting to a close and opens up a new chapter. We can learn a lot from the nativity about those moments that act as catalysts, and the dynamics of change in our own lives. But of course, the nativity only looks like that in retrospect: for the holy family at the time, a great deal of what we now consider hugely significant was, for them, everyday life. It is good to gain perspective on life by remembering that things that seem very ordinary to us are not necessarily unimportant.

[22 December]

Coming, ready or not…

In those days Mary set out and went with haste to a Judean town in the hill country, where she entered the house of Zechariah and greeted Elizabeth. When Elizabeth heard Mary's greeting, the child leapt in her womb. And Elizabeth was filled with the Holy Spirit and exclaimed with a loud cry, 'Blessed are you among women, and blessed is the fruit of your womb. And why has this happened to me, that the mother of my Lord comes to me? For as soon as I heard the sound of your greeting, the child in my womb leapt for joy. And blessed is she who believed that there would be a fulfilment of what was spoken to her by the Lord.'

LUKE 1:39–45

There's a sense of heightened excitement about this encounter between Mary and Elizabeth. The language Luke uses gives an exuberance to their meeting. His verbs give a lot of positive, forward-moving action: Mary *set out* and *went with haste*; Mary *entered*; the child *leapt*. Their conversation is not just in ordinary terms like 'she said…' but Mary *greeted* and Elizabeth *exclaimed with a loud cry*. To accompany the mental image of two pregnant women, several of the words also give a sense of being full: Mary *entered* the house; Elizabeth was *filled* with the Spirit; the child leapt *in her womb*, there is a *fulfilment* of what was spoken. The whole paragraph, then, creates a feeling of blessing, filling, joy and overflowing happiness.

There is another nice reversal in this paragraph. Elizabeth is from the priestly temple family, and well-to-do, while Mary is a poor rural girl. Yet it is Elizabeth who is bearing the prophet, and Mary who is bearing the king and priest. It is Elizabeth who bows before

Mary, in a foreshadowing of the relationship between John and Jesus, where John, the older cousin, will bow before Jesus. In addition to the prophetic quality of this encounter, there is an effervescence about it, which perhaps comes in part from our knowledge that no one except these two women really understood each other's situation.

They were at the very opposite ends of their childbearing potential. One had borne years and years of both the social stigma and the personal disappointment of childlessness; the other found herself expecting a baby before she even believed it possible. The age gap between them meant that Elizabeth could have been Mary's mother. Both women knew they were carrying children who were specially sent by God under extraordinary circumstances, but neither Mary nor Elizabeth were ready, in the practical sense, for a baby. We're given the impression that both women welcomed their babies gladly, but for each of them there were elements of serious inconvenience about the timing.

Elizabeth was well into middle age and had given up hope of ever having children. Even though she may have been overjoyed, she would surely have worried about the disruption this late baby would bring to her settled existence, to say nothing of her health. Even with the benefit of modern medicine, it isn't always plain sailing now to have a baby late in life. Back then, when it was common for either mother or child or both to die in childbirth, Elizabeth must have had moments of anxiety, wondering at the timing of this baby.

Mary, meanwhile, was only just betrothed, not even married. For her, the timing of events could hardly have been less convenient. She had not yet set up home with Joseph, her pregnancy would be regarded by many as scandalous and, in the middle of all this, she and Joseph had to embark on a long and tiring journey to be registered for tax.

When the grace and love of God invade our lives, it is rarely according to our timetables. When we think we need him, he is unbearably absent, and then, just when we feel that our hands are full, suddenly our cup is overflowing.

Just over ten years ago, I was a PhD student and an ordinand, taking two courses simultaneously, each with a deadline. Then I found that I was pregnant. I was blissfully happy about it: this was a baby I had longed for. All the same, my circumstances were undeniably less than ideal, and I spent some sleepless nights trying to figure out how to make all the pieces fit together. I needed to know how maternity leave worked for ordinands, what would happen about the bits of my course I would miss, and what to do about practical things like student grants and housing. I went to see my tutor, a kind and humorous woman who could be formidable when necessary, and together we discovered that, to date, there was no policy on maternity leave or funding breaks for pregnant ordinands. I don't think I was the first woman priest to have a baby mid-training, but there had been so few thus far that there wasn't any established pattern. I sat in my tutor's study while she phoned the relevant grant-awarding bodies, dioceses and central offices, trying to get some kind of game plan together. After a number of long, frustrating calls, I heard the mumble of a man's voice at the other end of the phone, and then my tutor's terse reply: 'It may well be that you don't have any policies. But what you don't seem to understand is that the birth of this baby cannot be postponed. This baby will be born in four months' time whether you have policies or not.'

I like the fact that the coming of God into our world was realized in something as inconvenient, unpredictable and untidy as the birth of a baby. A baby will be born when it's ready to be born. It makes no difference whether we are ready and, in any case, who is ever ready for a baby? But regardless of theologies and postmodern theories and new ideas of Church, and irrespective of our programmes and plans and energy levels, God will come and be born in our world.

Birth is a great leveller. It is always messy and inconvenient, painful and undignified. It is usually joyful, often frightening, sometimes tragic. It happens to those who are ready and those who are not. Babies break up the order of our lives and defy the plans of even the most organized of mothers-to-be. Birth isn't fair or controllable: it sometimes comes quickly and easily to people who are unprepared, and with agonized difficulty to those who have a meticulous birth plan.

So it is with God. He will be born in our world whether we're ready or not, deserving or not, prepared or not. The incarnation of God will defy our plans, upset the organized and come with ease and rapturous joy to undeserving sinners and the poor in spirit.

[23 December]

From now on…

And Mary said,
'My soul magnifies the Lord,
and my spirit rejoices in God my Saviour,
for he has looked with favour on the lowliness of his servant.
Surely, from now on all generations will call me blessed;
for the Mighty One has done great things for me,
and holy is his name.

LUKE 1:46–49

The fourth candle in the Advent wreath is lit to commemorate Mary, the mother of Jesus. Like the patriarchs, the prophets and John the Baptist, she too holds a special place in the story of salvation.

'My soul doth magnify the Lord' (v. 46, KJV). These are among the best-known words of scripture, so famous that even the infrequent churchgoer will recognize them. Like the Lord's Prayer and the 23rd Psalm, Mary's song is heard often enough to have the ring of familiarity about it. Traditionally sung at Vespers (evening prayer), the Magnificat was adopted into Evensong in the 1549 Book of Common Prayer, and has remained in every version of Evensong to the present day.

Theories vary as to exactly how the Magnificat came to be written. Perhaps it is a stylized version of what Mary herself really said, or it may be Luke's way of giving poetic expression to the meaning of the moment. There are strong similarities between the Magnificat and Hannah's song in 1 Samuel 2:1–10. Hannah was a woman who had waited and longed and prayed for a baby for many years before she had her son, Samuel. So it's interesting, given that Hannah's situation is much more like Elizabeth's than

Mary's, that a few early manuscripts attribute the Magnificat to Elizabeth.

Maybe the Magnificat was Luke's creation, or maybe Mary's, or perhaps Elizabeth really did say these words, partly quoting Hannah. However they came to be written, though, the Magnificat stands as a powerful poetic statement of the feeling and significance of these moments surrounding the incarnation of Christ. 'From now on…' (v. 48) is a phrase that deliberately looks forward, and the Magnificat as a whole is a song of hope. That's not to say that Mary anticipated a life of ease and constant celebration. There is a difference between wishing and hoping. Wishing is an unrealistic kind of idea—'If only I won the lottery, all my troubles would be over'—but hope is not dependent upon circumstances, and the joy it produces sustains people even when life is tough.

I was already very familiar with the Magnificat by the time I was ordained. I had heard it read or sung fairly often in church services, I'd done intensive studies on Luke's Gospel both at school and university, and I had preached sermons on it from time to time. But it wasn't until I became the chaplain at King's College Cambridge that I experienced daily Choral Evensong and heard the Magnificat and the Nunc Dimittis (Simeon's song from Luke 2) sung every evening, the musical setting changing each day but the words remaining exactly the same.

Hearing the same words day after day after day, their impact began, over time, to change. 'My soul doth magnify the Lord' I heard as I began in high spirits at the start of a new academic year, and my own soul seemed to sing along. 'He that is mighty has done great things for me, and holy is his name': such words are inspiring and apt when it seems that God is with you and all is well with the world. Who could not be grateful to be studying in a beautiful place with one of the best libraries in the world?

But the impact of the daily repetition of the Magnificat shifted for me when, after some months, a number of things in and around my world began to go very badly indeed. To the great shock of the whole world, the Twin Towers fell in New York. Shortly after that, a couple of serious personal misfortunes came my way. By the middle of that winter, an immense tiredness began to tell, which came from working too hard under difficult circumstances. Then those words seemed almost like a daily mockery. 'My soul doth magnify the Lord' sang the choir but, in my heart, I felt there was nothing to give thanks for. 'For he has looked with favour on the lowliness of his servant': well, 'lowly' I could relate to, but I couldn't see how I was in God's favour. 'He that is mighty has done great things for me': I could see that Mary felt that way, but in the wake of local and international disaster, it felt to me more as if God had forgotten me.

It was then that I discovered a new dynamic to the words of this ancient song. Until that time, I had always thought that I read the Bible, but now, somehow, in this daily experience of repetition, it suddenly seemed that it was reading me—not mocking me, after all, but calling me to a new understanding of God. It was calling me to discover what it means to say 'My soul doth magnify...' even when the presence of God is far away, and to believe that 'He who is mighty hath done great things for me' even when everything seems to be falling apart. Eventually I discovered a kind of defiance in the midst of doubt, a determination that I would honour God, seemingly against the odds, believing that somehow he would once again lift up the needy from the ash-heap.

Mary's song, then, may be joyful, but it is not triumphalistic. Her prophetic words pick up the theme of reversal again: her testimony that God blesses the poor is not an announcement that there will be no more poverty, but that God will reverse the expectations. She is still poor, but she now knows herself to be blessed by God.

So a song of praise like this can make sense even when things are not going well. We can adopt these words when our daily experience is disaster and death, not as a denial of reality but as a proclamation of hope. We noted a few days ago that in Mary's story permission to question God is writ large. Here in her Magnificat, there is also the challenge to adopt a stubborn, almost defiant belief—not blind faith, but a determination to let God set the agenda and not to give up faith too easily.

'From now on...' also seems to call to mind the journey of Abraham. There is all the difference in the world between stepping forward in a new beginning and 'abandoning' or cutting yourself off from your past. Abraham, and later Mary, lived with their traditions but looked forward and travelled hopefully. Like the patriarch's long journey from promise to fulfilment, Mary learned through the physical reality of bearing a child that it takes time to germinate new life. New things take time from promise to inception, from beginning to fulfilment.

We live in an 'instant' society: we can buy now and pay later, and the idea of saving and waiting and taking our time about decisions is diminished. There is something healthy about the enforced waiting of having a baby: it makes you pause to consider what is coming. There may be moments of regret over the loss of other interests, which will have to be abandoned or put aside to make time and space for a baby. There is a constantly shifting sense of personal identity as your size and shape, your role in the world and your place in the family home gradually change.

'From now on...' calls us to look forward positively while still living realistically in the present. It is a call to live with an eye to the future, not to escape the realities of everyday life but to give hope to the present.

[24 December]

Magnificat: a promise and a call

The Mighty One has done great things for me,
and holy is his name.
His mercy is for those who fear him
from generation to generation.
He has shown strength with his arm;
he has scattered the proud in the thoughts of their hearts.
He has brought down the powerful from their thrones,
and lifted up the lowly;
he has filled the hungry with good things,
and sent the rich away empty.

LUKE 1:49–53

The Magnificat, the song Mary sang when she went to see her cousin Elizabeth, is supremely a song of hope, beginning in praise and gratitude and developing into a prophetic anthem of justice. Mary's contemporaries would have recognized some of the words and phrases as being drawn from the traditions of scripture.

'He has lifted up the lowly; he has filled the hungry with good things, and sent the rich away empty.' Mary's words overturn the order of things. She admits that, realistically, poverty and injustice are part of life. Life isn't fair, and there is a certain amount of moral chaos that keeps it that way. Yet the Magnificat flows like a river of hope—Mary's vision of how things could be, in a world where the downtrodden are lifted up and the hungry are filled with good things.

The Magnificat has the same sort of dynamic as God's call to Abram did in Genesis 12, where God promised to lead him to a new land and give him descendants. But a promise that began as a personal blessing then flowed out to the whole world. Just as God promised to bless Abram so that 'all the families of the earth shall be blessed' (Genesis 12:3), so Mary's baby was not a blessing for her alone, but would bring justice and redemption to the whole world. The fact that the Magnificat echoes the traditions of ancient Israel—from 1 Samuel, Exodus and the prophet Isaiah—shows Jesus to be a continuation and fulfilment of those hopes.

But... whenever we read promises of justice like this in the Bible, inspiring and hopeful though they may be, it is impossible to ignore the fact that in Jesus' lifetime hunger and poverty were not eliminated and, even two millennia later, the world is still unfair: there is still injustice and poverty, sickness and hunger and death. So what do we make now of Mary's proclamation of justice? Do we say that it was a prophecy that didn't work out? Or do we say that Mary was just dreaming impossible dreams? Come to that, I wonder what Mary herself thought later, when Jesus' earthly life was over and poverty was still all around her? When she was old and grey, did Mary still believe that God had done great things for her, or did she change her mind?

I think that two things (at least!) help to make sense of the Magnificat as a song of justice that still speaks to us today. The first is to consider the life experience out of which Mary sang this song. There was no middle class in the first-century Middle East: most of the people were poor and worked hard for their daily bread. In addition, they were living under the occupation of a regime that thought nothing of demanding more and more taxes from people who couldn't afford them. Life was very tough and the regime unforgiving. The Magnificat does not read to me like the words of someone who accepts that there is nothing to do but wait for God to fix it: it sounds more like a statement of defiance in the face of injustice. This song has a fire in its guts.

I love the way the song gives a different side to Mary's character from the one we are used to. We have a great deal of exposure to the idea of Mary as meek and obedient and thoughtful. When the angel Gabriel visited her and broke the news that she was to become the mother of Christ, we are told that first Mary was perplexed, and then replied, 'Let it be with me according to your word' (Luke 1:38). Those words are usually read in a tone that suggests a rather subservient Mary, obeying just because she couldn't think what else to do. The Magnificat, though, has a quality of determination about it, a stubborn commitment to hope, in the language of political activism. So here we see Mary not in the classical religious mode of 'meek and mild', but seriously worked up about injustice and determined to see things change. I wonder, in fact, whether this feisty view of Mary is closer to the truth than the traditional image of a Mary who wouldn't say boo to a goose!

The second approach is to read the Magnificat in the context of the whole of Luke's Gospel. The Magnificat states boldly that salvation is about the whole of life, and doesn't allow us to separate spiritual matters into some ethereal place where neither life nor reason impinge upon them. It's about justice for the oppressed, light in the darkness, freedom for the enslaved. But Luke nowhere suggests that justice is going to be delivered miraculously and instantaneously by Jesus. Instead, he shows us a Jesus who teaches that the gospel cannot be a promise of justice unless it is understood also as a call to justice.

For instance, when Jesus preached on the mountainside (Luke 6), he started by saying, 'Blessed are you who are hungry now, for you shall be filled... Woe to you who are full now, for you will be hungry' (vv. 21, 25). Jesus, it seems, was teaching the same stuff that his mother had said before he was born, but he doesn't defer the promise of justice to the afterlife. Luke tells us that Jesus continued immediately with a call to action, for you and me to create justice here and now. Throughout his Gospel, Luke continually flags up his concern for the poor, often speaking of the 'orphan and the widow'. An orphan, back then, was not a child with no parents at all but a child with no father. The 'orphan and the widow' were a family that had no means of support and, unless people around them took care of them, they would be at least hungry, if not homeless and destitute. Some people think that when Luke did the research for his Gospel, he talked personally to Mary, and that this is why his Gospel is the only one with the inside story about the birth of Jesus. If this is true, perhaps it was Mary who pointed out to Luke how important it had been that people had cared for her and Jesus and his siblings when she was widowed. (It is generally assumed that Joseph died well before Jesus started his public ministry.)

James is another biblical writer who talks about the gospel in terms of practical justice. James' letter was famously disliked by Luther, who scathingly referred to it as an 'epistle of straw' on the basis that it didn't say very much specifically about the saving work of Christ. What James does say, though, loud and clear, is that the point of the gospel is justice. True religion, says James, is 'to care for orphans and widows in their distress' (1:27), and when he says 'God opposes the proud, but gives grace to the humble' (4:6), again we can hear echoes of the Magnificat.

Tradition has it that this letter was written by James the younger brother of Jesus, or possibly someone who was a close follower of James. That's an intriguing connection, given that James, like Luke, gives a strong emphasis to the orphan and widow. Could we be hearing actual memories of Mary's voice here? In any case, James takes the same point as Luke—justice—and bangs the nail home, saying bluntly that the gospel is neither an abstract faith nor a promise of God's intervention, but a call to practical activism. 'Feed the orphan and the widow,' says James, 'or you have no faith worth speaking of' (see James 1:27). If he were walking the streets of Britain today, he might well say, 'Take care of single mothers', and he'd probably also say, 'Give food and shelter to the homeless' or 'Take care of refugees.' We are the agents of God's kingdom. A faith that Jesus will fix things for us is, according to James, an empty faith. True faith in Jesus and in his gospel will spur us to action.

The Magnificat, then, is not a prophecy that didn't come true, nor a dream of utopia, but a vision of justice that demands an active response. The gospel isn't a promise unless it is also a call.

[25 December]

No room at the inn?

In those days a decree went out from Caesar Augustus, that a census be taken of all the inhabited earth. This was the first census taken while Quirinius was governor of Syria. And everyone was on his way to register for the census, each to his own city. Joseph also went up from Galilee, from the city of Nazareth, to Judea, to the city of David which is called Bethlehem, because he was of the house and family of David, in order to register along with Mary, who was engaged to him, and was with child. While they were there, the days were completed for her to give birth. And she gave birth to her firstborn son; and she wrapped him in cloths, and laid him in a manger, because there was no room for them in the inn.

LUKE 2:1–7 (NASB)

Some years ago, I went on a study trip to Israel to visit various ancient sites and archeological digs, to help put some historical flesh on the bones of the biblical accounts. I was, at the time, going through a massive rethink of the way I'd been educated in reading the Bible, and an opportunity like this was something to be cherished. One of the things that surprised and delighted me was that visiting these sites often challenged traditional interpretations of the biblical stories. The Christmas stories are a case in point. Christmas cards and nativity plays leave us with an image of starlight, snow, a lonely family in a strange place, ending up spending the night in a freezing cold and delapidated wooden stable, rejected by all and sundry, callously put out in the street in their moment of greatest need. But a little knowledge of the geography of the area and the customs of the time suggest a somewhat different interpretation.

Mary and Joseph, we are told, went to Bethlehem to take part in a census. Why Bethlehem? Because it was where their family originated—not a town in which they were complete strangers but a place where their relatives still lived, and any other relatives who had migrated would also have been returning. So the idea that they were isolated foreigners in a strange town is a little wide of the mark.

The layout of a first-century house in the Middle East also gives the lie to the idea of their being banished to a freezing stable. The word we translate as 'inn' is *kataluma*, which is not a hotel or B&B let out to strangers, but a large family living room used for eating and for receiving guests. If there were a lot of guests, they would eat, drink, talk, laugh and socialize well into the night, then just roll out the blankets on the floor and bunk down to sleep—the whole roomful, children and all. The domestic animals were not far from the scene either. In a small, one-storey house, they would have been kept in a room within the house itself, but in Bethlehem there is a series of caves below the ground, forming a kind of basement to the houses, which were probably used for housing animals. One of these caves is kept as the actual birthplace of Jesus. It is impossible to prove whether or not it really is the precise location, but it might as well be, given that Bethlehem is a small and compact place. If it wasn't that particular cave, it would have been an identical one within a few hundred metres. The caves are constantly warm and dry throughout the year—over 16 degrees Celsius—so if Jesus was born in Bethlehem among the family's domestic animals, then it was not in a freezing wooden shed at the bottom of the garden but in a warm, dry shelter within the family home.

The layout of the house and the likelihood that Mary and Joseph found themselves among relatives give a somewhat different spin to the Christmas story—but a no less challenging one to our faith. Imagine, if you will, that first Christmas. Because of the census, numerous people whose family origins were in Bethlehem were converging on this very small town, so small that it had no inns. While the census itself was no cause for celebration, an enforced family party was inevitably going to lighten the atmosphere. The house with the biggest *kataluma*—living room, dining room and guest room—would naturally play host to the party. Perhaps aunties and grannies from down the road would bring dessert and salads, and maybe put up a few extra guests. The *kataluma* would have been chock-full of people, from the smallest babies to the oldest pensioners, eating, drinking, chatting, laughing, crying, catching up on the news. Then, as the noise levels begin to rise, there's another knock at the door. Mary and Joseph arrive, and Mary is almost immediately in labour. If you have a one-roomed house already packed to the rafters, with children everywhere and people preparing to sleep there in a few hours' time, where do you put a woman who goes into labour? There really was no room in the *kataluma*, but downstairs there was a warm, dry, quiet space—the stable.

How well Mary and Joseph knew their relatives, we can't be sure, and neither can we know quite how much of a shadow was cast by Mary's condition. It's not clear from the biblical accounts whether the expected child was a public disgrace or merely an initial threat to Joseph, as he was sure the baby was not naturally his own child. So we can't be sure whether they received a warm, affectionate welcome or a bit of a frosty one. We don't know whether the stable was offered as an act of pure kindness to a couple in need, or somewhat grudgingly, out of family obligation. The stable might have represented a rejection of the holy family by their relatives—putting them in a safe but out-of-the-way space, not wanting to go to the bother of disturbing the rest of the household for these relatives of questionable morality. Equally, the stable could have been the best thing a family of moderate means could offer.

No room in the *kataluma*. We too may be of moderate means. In spiritual terms, we may not be able to offer Jesus a dwelling-place fit for a king. We may have only the spiritual equivalent of a one-roomed house, the central space in our lives already overflowing with all manner of events and people that demand our attention. Maybe we were not ready for his arrival, either. Maybe the best we have to offer is a bit of an improvization—a stumbling, inadequate welcome, but something equivalent to hurriedly sweeping out a space in the warm, dry stable—not luxury, just the best we can do for now. But do you know what? Jesus doesn't ask us to sweep out our lives before he will be born within us. He asks only that we find whatever space we can, and do not delay, because his birth (and our rebirth) is imminent. He doesn't wait for a rapturous and well-prepared welcome. He won't turn down our humble, imperfect and perhaps even slightly grudging invitation. He doesn't ask for satin and velvet, diamonds and Dom Perignon. He'll be born wherever. All we have to do is make a space for him.

[26 December]

Dirty or clean

The angel said to [the shepherds], 'Do not be afraid; for see—I am bringing you good news of great joy for all the people: to you is born this day in the city of David a Saviour, who is the Messiah, the Lord. This will be a sign for you: you will find a child wrapped in bands of cloth and lying in a manger.'

LUKE 2:10–12

In places where animals are kept, there is a lot of hay and straw. Straw is spread about on the floor to soak up the mess and the dirt. But fresh, clean hay, sweet smelling and softer than straw, is put in the feeding stalls. When Jesus was born, they laid him in the cleanest corner of the stable—the manger full of fresh, clean hay. People always put babies in the cleanest environment they can create. The manger may sound somewhat precarious to us, because we are used to easy access to boiled water and sterilizing equipment and washing machines. A feeding stall is a far cry from the standards of cleanliness in a maternity hospital, but it was the best they could do.

It's not surprising, either, that Jesus was swaddled—wrapped up very firmly in long strips of cloth to make him safe and keep his limbs close to his body. We don't swaddle babies in 21st-century England, but we often do something similar, wrapping a frustrated baby tightly and firmly in blankets and holding him very still so that he will come to peace and sleep. I remember being taught to wrap my son very snugly in a blanket to stop the 'startle reflex'—a kind of jerking of the arms and legs in response to cold, draughts or noise or anything else that is upsetting and distressing for tiny babies. Wrapping them up snugly helps them to calm down and feel safe.

Jesus was born into our world in order to become totally redemptively involved in the mess and chaos, the dirt and distress. It's a nice irony, then, that the first thing they did to Jesus was to wrap him up as tightly as possible to make him safe and warm and quiet, and lay him down in the cleanest available environment. Here is another example of the idea of reversal. We expect Jesus to be where it's clean, but he is born into the mess of human life. We think of Jesus as safe and calm and serene, but he grows up to be the kind of leader who has his sleeves rolled up, ready to face reality and connect the spiritual world to the material one. We try to restrain him and keep him clean, but he breaks out of those expectations. Our idea of 'holy' is to protect God from anything unpleasant and unmentionable, yet Jesus' idea of 'holy' is to bring the fresh air of heaven right into the dirtiest and messiest corners of our world. He will not remain restrained, swaddled, safe, warm and still for very long.

Of course, swaddling cloths and clean hay were the right things to provide for a baby at that time, yet there is a parallel here with our faith. The Christian faith is, in every way, one that thoroughly and uncompromisingly integrates the spiritual with the physical. There is no dualism in Christianity: one of the central ideas of incarnation is that there is no privileging of the spiritual over the physical. God is born into a physical body in a physical world, not to save us from our bodies or from the world we live in, but to redeem us within our humanity as physical beings. We, by contrast, seem to carry an instinct to separate body from soul. We don't readily associate God with the mess of everyday life, the realities of physical existence. We prefer to sanitize the world for God. Our instinctive reaction to all things holy is to make a holy space for them—to keep them protected from the vile and the shameful, the dirty and unacceptable parts of our world and our lives. But however much we attempt this sanitization process, the real God will break right out of the protective swaddlings, jump out of the nice clean manger and be down in the dirt before we can stop him.

[27 December]

The Word became flesh

In the beginning was the Word, and the Word was with God, and the Word was God. He was in the beginning with God. All things came into being through him, and without him not one thing came into being. What has come into being in him was life, and the life was the light of all people. The light shines in the darkness, and the darkness did not overcome it…

And the Word became flesh and lived among us, and we have seen his glory, the glory as of a father's only son, full of grace and truth. (John testified to him and cried out, 'This was he of whom I said, "He who comes after me ranks ahead of me because he was before me."') From his fullness we have all received, grace upon grace. The law indeed was given through Moses; grace and truth came through Jesus Christ. No one has ever seen God. It is God the only Son, who is close to the Father's heart, who has made him known.

JOHN 1:1–5, 14–18

Through the course of this book, we've seen how the Advent wreath highlights some key characters in the unfolding story of salvation. We saw that the first candle on the wreath represents the patriarchs, beginning with Abraham and his descendants. Abraham heard God calling to him from beyond the curtain of stars, and he and his family set out on a journey to find something more beyond the horizon, a dream of a better life in a better place, propelled by God's promise of a land they could call their own. The promise was focused on a place. Once they arrived in Canaan, though, they realized that the land alone was not the sum total of the promise. Perhaps like people in fairy stories who go to big cities to find streets paved with gold, Abraham's family discovered that all the troubles of life travelled to Canaan with them—climate problems and natural disasters, political conflicts with their neighbours, internal strife within the family as it expanded. In the whole of the Old Testament historical narratives, you can barely find five minutes of peace. The land was wonderful in many ways, but the place alone did not fulfil the promise.

Time passed, and the prophets, for whom we lit the second candle, began to retell the story. They pointed out to the ancient Israelites the error of their ways, rebuked them for their internal squabbles and their political wrangling, and warned of trouble ahead. They predicted the same outcome that befalls every great civilization—that just when they think they are king of the world, it all comes tumbling down. When the great invasions came, in the seventh and sixth centuries BC, Israel was torn apart: the rich, the skilled and the educated were taken into captivity, leaving behind a poverty-stricken population in a decimated land. Both at home and in exile, there were prophets who continued to look forward to a time when the promises of God would be fulfilled, a time in the future when wrongs would be made right, the people would be reunited and life would be framed by justice and filled with peace. The prophets, then, shifted the focus from a place to a time. The promised land became less a literal location than a metaphor for the life they dreamed of at a future time when God would restore them. The dream of the future also gained a special focus in the shape of a mythical figure, a Messiah, who would be sent by God to save his people, his arrival heralded by another kind of prophet—someone who would seem to be like Elijah.

This second Elijah-figure eventually materialized in the person of John the Baptist, for whom we lit the third Advent candle. By this time, the land was occupied by the Romans, and the people were longing for political freedom. They expected John to bring them a Messiah who would win political freedom and independence as a nation. John the Baptist did have some characteristics reminiscent of Elijah: he lived as a recluse in the desert, ate raw foods like insects and honey, and dressed in a style so far from fashionable that it was on the edge of unacceptable. But he didn't deliver them a political revolutionary for a Messiah, or even a miraculous one. He began to talk not about a Messiah who was coming from heaven, but one who was already there among them. 'He is one of you,' said John. 'You don't recognize him, but he's right here among you.'

It must have been baffling! You can imagine the people looking round and wondering which of them could possibly be the Messiah. Surely it would be someone highly educated, or with great business acumen, or perhaps plenty of respect in the community—a judge, a lawyer, or a rabbi? The last person they would think of would be a chippie from the local builders, especially not one whose paternity was in question. But John changed the expectation of the people: instead of anticipating a Messiah from somewhere beyond, they needed to look for a Messiah in the midst—a God down here instead of a God out there.

The fourth candle on the wreath, lit for Mary the mother of Jesus, intensifies the image even further, because she shows us a Messiah who is not just among us but within us. Through revelation and personal experience, Mary understood that God wanted to be more than near us: he wanted to dwell within our very being. For Mary, uniquely, that meant physically carrying a child. For the rest of us, the image of her bearing the Christ-child is a metaphor for the spiritual reality of our new birth—not an external miracle but an inner transformation.

The opening of John's Gospel at first seems to speak of the Word of God as being in another place and time, far away in a dimension we can't touch or imagine or understand. The Word was with God—*was* God—from the very beginning, and, as John reminds us, no one has ever seen God. But the Word became flesh and dwelt among us: he became like us, within us, one of us. The mystery of the incarnation is that God is made flesh, but its clarity is that now we can see and touch and feel and understand.

Like the patriarchs and prophets and the followers of John the Baptist, we sometimes imagine that salvation is waiting for us in another place or at another time, or that it will be brought by a person we have not yet met but who will change our lives for the better. People who long for more to life may pin their hopes on such things—sometimes in a realistic way, such as planning to move to a new town or job or country, but sometimes falling into a fantasy world of lottery wins or knights in shining armour.

The extraordinary thing, though, about the salvation that God sends in Jesus is how ordinary it is. The transforming power of God, when we actually encounter it, seems less dramatic than a promised land, less ethereal than a future time, and less exotic than a superhero saviour. Sometimes we try to grasp our salvation by focusing on Jesus as out-of-the-ordinary, by thinking of his deity, of the extraordinary circumstances of his birth or the world-changing impact of his life and his teachings. But to think of salvation as something far away, in another place or time, keeps it at arm's length from us and refuses to grasp what really happened—that God spoke, in the end, in a way that placed salvation right here in ordinary everyday life. 'And the Word became flesh and dwelt among us' (v. 14). A God who is born as one of us is more ordinary than exotic but, in the end, more real and effective, because he transforms us, slowly but surely, from the inside out.

[28 December]

Joseph

Now the birth of Jesus the Messiah took place in this way. When his mother Mary had been engaged to Joseph, but before they lived together, she was found to be with child from the Holy Spirit. Her husband Joseph, being a righteous man and unwilling to expose her to public disgrace, planned to dismiss her quietly. But just when he had resolved to do this, an angel of the Lord appeared to him in a dream and said, 'Joseph, son of David, do not be afraid to take Mary as your wife, for the child conceived in her is from the Holy Spirit. She will bear a son, and you are to name him Jesus, for he will save his people from their sins.' All this took place to fulfil what had been spoken by the Lord through the prophet: 'Look, the virgin shall conceive and bear a son, and they shall name him Emmanuel', which means, 'God is with us.'

MATTHEW 1:18–23

Some of the stories surrounding the birth of Jesus are nothing less than fantastic. Angelic appearances and strange patterns in the stars and people being struck dumb—this is out-of-the-ordinary, dramatic stuff. But we have two stories in which Joseph hears a direct message from God, and both times it comes in the more everyday mode of dreams. Why would God speak in dreams to Joseph and not send angels? Perhaps each person was given a mode of communication that was right for them.

We don't know much about Joseph. Matthew's is the only Gospel that gives us a glimpse of the birth story from Joseph's point of view, and even here there isn't much detail—but there are a few things that we can glean about Joseph by reading between the lines.

The first thing that emerges from this passage is that Joseph was a merciful and kind man. Discovering that Mary was pregnant with a child that wasn't his would automatically lead to his cancelling the marriage. Joseph was also within his rights, according to the law, to have her stoned to death for her betrayal—but he didn't do that. Instead, he decided simply to end the betrothal quietly and not see Mary harmed. He was betrayed, or so it seemed, but he was benevolent and not vengeful towards Mary, even before God spoke to him in his dream.

Joseph must also have been a man of rather unusual humility. His dream gave him a personal reassurance that Mary had not betrayed him with another man, but that didn't alter the fact that taking Mary as his wife under these circumstances would mean living with public gossip about whose baby it was, and perhaps losing honour and respect in his own community. The dream came as an invitation from God. Would Joseph be willing to take Mary as his wife and raise the baby as his own? Just as Mary had the possibility of saying 'no' to becoming the child's mother, there was no obligation on Joseph to act as his father. We shouldn't overlook the magnitude of Joseph's decision in saying 'yes' to God and to Mary. It was an act of human kindness and everyday courage, and these human qualities turned out to be just as important as supernatural events in bringing God's Son into the world.

Keeping hold of the interaction between heaven and earth—the combination of human ordinariness and strange events—is hard to do when we read the birth stories. Too often, we overemphasize one or the other. If we focus always on the spectacular and the extraordinary, we can miss the down-to-earth aspects of the story. Then we can begin to believe that we connect with God only in a space that is slightly outside our everyday existence. The heart of the story is that God became like us so that we could become like him. God took on human form so that the image of God could be restored and fulfilled in us. As the Collect for Christmas puts it, 'Grant that, as he came to share in our humanity, so we may share the life of his divinity.'[3]

The Gospels tend to portray Joseph as a quiet background figure in the story, but I think that paying attention to him helps us to 'earth' the story, and gives it the context of everyday reality. Joseph's vital contribution to bringing God's Son into the world was entirely within the realm of ordinariness—not angels, but plain dreams; not a miraculous conception, but solid acts of human kindness and generosity. Mary's 'yes' to God highlights the heavenly intervention of God into our world. Joseph's 'yes' is a picture of simple human goodness, a reception of God into the everyday.

'They shall name him Emmanuel' (v. 23): God is with us, not requiring us to be more than human. He is with us in the ordinariness of everyday life and requires only that, within that ordinariness, we say our 'yes' to him.

[29 December]

Fear, worship and wide-eyed wonder

And suddenly there was with the angel a multitude of the heavenly host, praising God and saying, 'Glory to God in the highest heaven, and on earth peace among those whom he favours!' When the angels had left them and gone into heaven, the shepherds said to one another, 'Let us go now to Bethlehem and see this thing that has taken place, which the Lord has made known to us.' So they went with haste and found Mary and Joseph, and the child lying in the manger. When they saw this, they made known what had been told them about this child; and all who heard it were amazed at what the shepherds told them. But Mary treasured all these words and pondered them in her heart. The shepherds returned, glorifying and praising God for all they had heard and seen, as it had been told them.

LUKE 2:13–20

We read on 21 December that the shepherds were faced at first with just one angel, who began his announcement in a way that is customary for angels: 'Do not be afraid.' It's fair to assume that being met by an angel might make anyone afraid, but after being frightened by one solitary being, wouldn't a whole sky full of angels praising God seem far more alarming? The descriptions we have of angelic visitations are indeed pretty scary! School nativity play interpretations of the story of a baby born in the night among doe-eyed cattle and soft-skinned donkeys give us a completely benevolent image of angels as lightweight, girlie creatures who wouldn't hurt a fly. But remember that when Zechariah saw an angel, 'he was terrified; and fear overwhelmed him' (Luke 1:12).

And the shepherds are also described as 'terrified' at the sight of the first angel (2:9). 'Do not be afraid', then, seems a good opening line for an angel.

I was told as a young child that the phrase 'Fear not' appears 366 times in the Bible—one for every day of even the longest year. I haven't counted, but the phrase does, without doubt, capture something at the very heart of the story of the incarnation. God is so holy, so pure in his goodness, that the sense of his presence has always left people rapt with wonder and awe. Moses begged God to let him see his face, but even the sight of God's retreating back was almost too much for him, and his own face shone with such neon brilliance as a result that other people couldn't bear to look at him afterwards (Exodus 33:17–23; 34:29–30).

Yet, as every parent, every child and every lover knows, you need to be able to look your beloved straight in the face. Someone you speak to but never encounter physically is always remote and 'other'. The incarnation is God's resolution: God, who is 'other', becomes one of us. We cannot look into the face of God but we can look into the face of Jesus. The baby in the manger has no need to say 'Fear not'. Despite the fact that most first-time parents go through moments of panic, babies are not terrifying or awesome in the same way that angels are. The knowledge of their complete dependence on us is frightening, but not the child itself, and the child in the manger does not inspire terror through his superior and unfamiliar power. Instead, he inspires wonder, love and careful attention, as he simply requires that we love him. Elizabeth Goudge once wrote that 'if a very important person frightens you, he is not great, he only thinks he is'.[4] Truly great people rise above the need to impress others with how great they are. Thus God, in Jesus Christ, completes the picture of his love to us—the paradox being that the awe-inspiring, utterly transcendent God can also look upon us from the face of a helpless child.

The shepherds, then, hearing the announcement of the first Christmas, are frightened at first, but once they have taken in the news, the sight of the heavenly host seems to galvanize them into action. Afraid at first, they are now excited and energetic. They don't fall down in wonder, they don't question or take time to ponder, they don't argue back and they don't react with unbelieving cynicism. They simply believe the news and act on it. 'Let us go... and see this thing that has taken place,' they say to one another (v. 15)—not to see whether it's true, not to see whether the angels were really talking in metaphors. They just take the message at face value.

Running off to find the baby, the shepherds do not become prophets, mute fathers of heralds, or mothers of Messiahs. They just become simple, straightforward worshippers. But having become worshippers, they also become witnesses, telling everyone in earshot what they had heard and seen. Sometimes we make the business of sharing faith far too complicated, as if we need to be world experts in the subject before we can open our mouths. We don't need to know anything much, really. We can just say what happened. That's what the shepherds did, and Luke tells us that 'all who heard it were amazed at what the shepherds told them' (v. 18).

I love the uncomplicated immediacy of the shepherds' response to the first Christmas. I love the way they take the news at face value, go and check it out, and then unashamedly tell everyone what they have seen, without fear for their respectability or credibility. Perhaps it's the case that those who have the least to lose find it easiest to receive.

One person in the story, though, had a different kind of reaction. Mary, the mother of Jesus, had known for some time that the baby she was carrying was special and different, although it's unlikely that she had any clear idea of exactly what that was going to mean. By the time the story was written down, of course, the storytellers had the hindsight to be able to tell the story as if Mary had known and understood in advance the significance of these extraordinary events. But reading between the lines, it seems that this was not quite the case. I think the story reads more as if the meaning of events became clear to Mary over time. She took Gabriel's announcement with cautious questioning, and here, for the second time, we are told that she 'pondered'. Luke says that Mary 'treasured all these words and pondered them in her heart' (v. 19), which suggests that she understood gradually the significance of what was happening around her. As we read on 19 December, 'ponder' means to weigh up or consider. Pondering doesn't lead to quick conclusions; it is the sort of thinking to which you keep coming back over a long period of time. Mary had already been thinking for some months about the significance of this baby; now she took in the shepherds' account of the angelic message, and afterwards she went on considering what it all meant. In fact, if you read to the end of the story, you will find that Mary was among the women present at Jesus' death, still trying to make sense of it all (John 19:25).

It's easy to say that the meaning of Christmas is peace on earth and goodwill to all people, but what will that mean to us by the middle of January? The Christmas message can end up sounding rather sweet and sentimental, turning Jesus into a baby who doesn't cry and the angels into floaty fairies who sing sweet songs rather than majestic creatures who scare the life out of people. It's easy to talk about peace on earth without even understanding how to have peace at home for a day and a half, or to say 'God is with us' without taking in the far-reaching implications of such an idea. So what does Christmas really mean?

I think it means a lot of things that are quite complex and difficult to unravel. It means that God, who could seem distant and unreal, became as real and immediate as a hungry, crying baby who simply cannot be ignored and completely disrupts every part of life. It means that God, whom we traditionally think of as all-powerful, becomes a powerless child who would rather relinquish his power than live in splendid isolation from those whom he loves. And ultimately, the meaning of Christmas is that God loves us so much, he cannot bear to live without us: a formula that takes a few seconds to say but suggests a depth of love that takes a lifetime to understand. Like Mary, we need to add all the pieces together, weighing and thinking about them deeply over a period of time, pondering them in our hearts.

During the Christmas festivities, many of us will be enjoying the company of friends and family, eating and drinking good things, giving and receiving presents, experiencing some days of fun and laughter. We might also, like the shepherds, feel a wide-eyed excitement at the wonder of it all, and hope for the peace and goodwill that they dreamed of. But a few days later, let's be sure we don't just close the book on Christmas for another year. If, like Mary, we ponder these things in our hearts throughout the year and throughout our lives, we will give ourselves the chance to discover how to make the love, peace, goodwill and childlike wonder of Christmas a reality in our own lives, in our families, in our communities, and in our world.

[30 December]

The man who is God

Let the same mind be in you that was in Christ Jesus,
who, though he was in the form of God,
did not regard equality with God
as something to be exploited,
but emptied himself,
taking the form of a slave,
being born in human likeness.
And being found in human form,
he humbled himself
and became obedient to the point of death—
even death on a cross.

Therefore God also highly exalted him
and gave him the name
that is above every name,
so that at the name of Jesus
every knee should bend,
in heaven and on earth and under the earth,
and every tongue should confess
that Jesus Christ is Lord,
to the glory of God the Father.

PHILIPPIANS 2:5–11

This beautiful passage, delivered to us by Paul in his letter to the Philippians, may have been Paul's own composition or it may have been an existing early Christian hymn that he was quoting to illustrate his point. We've looked at the idea of reversal in a number of places in this book. Here, perhaps better than anywhere in the

New Testament, Paul shows how the coming of Jesus into our world turns things upside down.

Through 2000 years of Christian history, a great deal of thought and energy (and paper) has been used in trying to understand and explain what it could possibly mean for Jesus to be both human and divine. Like many areas of Christian thought, we have to admit that ultimately it is a mystery, yet we still need to wrestle with the idea in order to make reasonable sense of our faith. But sometimes the desire to find a logical answer to the puzzle of the human and divine natures of Christ has become so intense that the purpose of the incarnation—for God to make himself known to us in Christ—has got somewhat lost in the mix. Surely God did not send his Son in order that we should have more practice at logic problems, but in order that we might have life.

Karl Rahner, a Jesuit priest and theologian writing in the mid-20th century, tried to avoid falling into the trap of creating an equation that allowed for God to assume a human identity without becoming less-than-God. Instead, Rahner approached the idea by saying that the dynamic of self-emptying (the theological term for this is *kenosis*) made it possible for God both to empty himself of himself and to take on a human nature. Therefore, God-in-Christ was not a compromise of two natures but an inherently creative and redemptive act. This act of self-emptying, said Rahner, was a true expression of what God is like. The Philippians hymn seems to suggest that Jesus had the choice whether or not to empty himself. Although he did act in freedom, the choice he made was an inevitable one—a 'no-brainer', if you like, because not to have done it would have been a failure of love. God is love, and therefore it is impossible for him to act in any way that is not love.

Paul calls us here to emulate Jesus in this self-emptying act of sacrifice: 'Let the same mind be in you that was in Christ Jesus' (v. 5). But it's important to make a distinction between service and subservience. As a number of liberation theologians have pointed out, in order to empty yourself you need to have a self in the first place, and we should beware, both for ourselves and for those around us, that we don't turn the idea of servanthood into something abusive. For the person who has no sense of self-worth, serving others in the name of Christ can be a journey into slavery, not sainthood, so we need to treat the idea of self-emptying with extreme care.

The distinction is clear in the story of Jesus washing the disciples' feet (John 13:3–15). If Jesus had actually been a servant, people would barely have noticed that their feet were being washed. When you pass through airport security, you don't usually take a lot of notice of the security staff. Your attention is focused on catching the plane on time, so, beyond perfunctory politeness, you don't have any cause to engage with the staff. Because they are uniformed and because they are carrying out a task that is part of the conveyor belt of travelling, they all seem to melt into one, just as, presumably, the travellers look pretty much the same to them. But supposing the Prime Minister walked up to you at airport security, offered to put your bags through the scanner for you and then carried them to the plane, you would certainly notice. Why would a person wielding that much power be looking after you? That is something like the shock of Jesus' action in washing the disciples' feet. Because it was Jesus, who was so important, doing a very menial task for them, he showed that the answer to the abuse of power is not to give it up, or to deny that you have it, but to use it to empower others. For us, then, our service of others and of God is not a means of validating ourselves or gaining an identity. It's the other way round. We, like Jesus, need to discover our validation first in relationship to God, and then, in self-emptying, serve the world because not to do so would be a failure of love.

In Philippians 2:5–11, it is puzzling that Jesus seems to be even 'higher' at the end than he was at the beginning. This defies logic entirely, for how can God be higher than God? Despite the mystery of the picture, though, it sets the pattern that we are then to follow: he emptied himself of all that he was in his godlike state, and became like us—with this purpose: that we can become like him. In Christian doctrine, this does not mean that we become God, but it does mean something more than simply being restored to a pre-fallen state. Redemption does not take us backwards to a state of innocence, but forwards, going beyond merely mending something that was broken, to offer us a vision of humanity that is greater than it was before.

The 'man who is God' turns himself inside out, empties himself for us. But the result is that we are given a vision of hope for humanity that exceeds our dreams. This is the purpose of incarnation and all that follows.

[SECTION 6]

Endings [and new beginnings]

In the first section, we saw that the way a story is begun affects the understanding of everything that follows. The same could be said of endings: once you have read the end of a book, it affects the way you reflect on everything you have read thus far. A happy ending, an ambiguous ending, a twist in the tale or an incomplete ending will all nuance the way in which a story is interpreted.

Fairy tales sometimes end with 'happily ever after', as if there is nothing more to tell. Most novels, though, leave hints in their endings that the story continues. What happens next may be the stuff of a sequel or it may be left to the reader's imagination, but the endings of most stories are never completely closed. In this section, we'll look at the way endings are presented in the biblical narratives—the ending of a Gospel, the closing chapters of the lives of two elderly people, the end of Jesus' earthly life, and the end of the Christmas story. We will see that, both in the biblical narrative and in the reality of our lives, endings are almost always the point of departure for new beginnings.

[31 December]

The end is where we started

[endings and Mark]

When the sabbath was over, Mary Magdalene, and Mary the mother of James, and Salome bought spices, so that they might go and anoint him. And very early on the first day of the week, when the sun had risen, they went to the tomb. They had been saying to one another, 'Who will roll away the stone for us from the entrance to the tomb?' When they looked up, they saw that the stone, which was very large, had already been rolled back. As they entered the tomb, they saw a young man, dressed in a white robe, sitting on the right side; and they were alarmed. But he said to them, 'Do not be alarmed; you are looking for Jesus of Nazareth, who was crucified. He has been raised; he is not here. Look, there is the place they laid him. But go, tell his disciples and Peter that he is going ahead of you to Galilee; there you will see him, just as he told you.' So they went out and fled from the tomb, for terror and amazement had seized them; and they said nothing to anyone, for they were afraid.

MARK 16:1–8

We started December by exploring the idea that the way books begin affects the way the whole book is understood, setting the scene and establishing little clues as to the sense of what follows. But the way that books end is also very important to the interpretation of the whole. The end may deliberately wrap up an issue or explain its meaning, it might resolve tensions or mysteries in the plot, or it might leave ideas or plotlines unresolved, hanging in the air like questions that the reader must answer.

Some books end so definitely, so clearly, that there is a satisfying sense of closure to the story. When the novel becomes fully fledged as a literary form, in the 19th century, we find many examples of stories in which complex threads of plot are satisfyingly tied up in the closing pages, the puzzles explained and the characters settled. Jane Austen, for example, usually left her heroines with all their outstanding worries resolved.

Later, though, novelists began to play with the form. An unresolved ending highlights the idea that all stories continue after the last page of the book: 'what happens next...?' is an eternal question. Another device, a twist in the tale, can reveal a piece of information in the last few pages that suddenly and dramatically shifts the interpretation of the entire story. The twist may take us back to the beginning of the book—either literally or to revisit the plot mentally—compelling us to rethink the unfolding plot and its meanings in the light of the unexpected revelation within the ending.

The 66 books of the Bible give us a variety of endings, some more intriguing than others. There are examples of letters that are very elegantly completed, leaving the reader in no doubt that the writer has finished the message. Take Jude, for instance, a letter that is absolutely conclusive, both in style and in content, with the closing sentences summing up the ultimate meaning of absolutely everything. There is no temptation to turn the page, wondering whether there will be a postscript or extra material, as there isn't really anything else to write.

The closing verses of Mark's Gospel are a different matter. The end of Mark is, in fact, quite a mystery. For a start, in an almost postmodern twist, we have a choice of three different endings. Verse 8, where we stopped reading today, is the point where the most ancient manuscripts come to a close. As you will have noticed, finishing the reading here means that there is something crucial missing from the Christian story! Mark gives us a rumour of something interesting that might have happened following the death of Jesus, but there is no clear account of a resurrection.

Two further, optional endings are added to Mark's Gospel. The second ending is simply an editorial sentence, just to show that that's the end of the manuscript. But the third option is a longer ending, a further twelve verses (vv. 9–20) that seem to finish off the story properly. (You might like to read those for yourself later.) Most scholars think that both these two extra endings were added later, in an attempt to correct the inconclusive ending that Mark had written.

Now of course, as every good student knows, an essay must have a beginning, a middle and an end! Many a promising piece of work has been docked of precious marks because it ends abruptly, with no suitable conclusion. If you're writing in an attempt to deliver an argument, you simply must have an ending. But Mark wasn't sitting an exam or writing an essay, and I think the editors and interpreters of the Bible have blurred an important feature of Mark's Gospel by insisting on finishing his book for him.

There are plenty of examples of books with strange or inconclusive endings. *The French Lieutenant's Woman* by John Fowles,[5] for instance, has three possible endings, which leave the reader to conclude the story, and allow for the idea that the author does not control the characters. Some time later, the fantasy writer Douglas Adams was among the first to envisage the possibility of the interactive online book, in which the reader's choices at various stages in a story would affect the way the plot developed and, eventually, how it ended.

As well as works with ambiguous endings, there are books and poems that actually have no ending at all: they just break off abruptly. Coleridge's poem 'Kubla Khan' is a good example of how this works as a literary technique. 'Kubla Khan' tells the story of a fantastic paradise, full of beautiful things and fascinating people. Then, just as the poem builds up to a really mysterious point, and just as you're waiting for the punchline, it breaks off tantalizingly and you never find out what happened next. Coleridge's own account of why he never finished the poem is often printed along with the poem itself. He claims that he saw the vision in a dream, but that as he was writing it down there was a knock at the door, and a visitor who came from Porlock interrupted him for more than an hour. When he went back to his writing, he couldn't recapture his vision, so the poem was left incomplete.

Some readers believed this story, and others thought it was just an excuse for Coleridge's procrastination. But maybe the visitor from Porlock was Coleridge's invention, created to represent the true reasons for writing a poem without an ending. The 19th-century Romantics believed it was possible to catch sight of a world beyond this one—a world of the spirit, that could not be fully understood but could be glimpsed in part. Coleridge's story of the visitor represents the fact that we are rooted firmly in the physical realm and cannot simply dissolve ourselves into the 'other' world. But that doesn't mean that the spiritual world is not real: it simply means that our understanding of it will only ever be partial. So Coleridge's poem has no ending exactly because we never can tell the whole story of the spiritual world: we can glimpse it but we cannot grasp it.

Fragmentary endings might tell us something about the meaning of the whole story, then. What's missing might be just as important in giving meaning to a text as what's there. But Mark, the Gospel writer, was not a Romantic, so why does his Gospel include no resurrection? Why does he stop at the point where Jesus' dead body is missing, without telling us that Jesus has risen? Why does he create a rumour and not turn it into a certainty?

I think there is actually something subtle and clever about this ending. It seems to me that Mark is putting the story right into the hands of the reader. Clear statements that Jesus rose from the dead, leaving no physical body behind him, have given rise to all sorts of efforts to 'prove', one way or another, what really happened, and to explain the implications of a resurrection. But Mark doesn't claim a resurrection: he simply hints at a mysterious event and leaves the matter hanging in the air. Maybe he had the foresight to realize that arguments and experiments would distract people from the real point of the story—which is that, if Jesus is alive, the significance of this fact must be to do with transforming our lives rather than our history books.

The story with an ambiguous or fragmentary ending, as we have seen, takes the reader back to the start of the book, to search out the missing clues or read again with a different perspective. In the case of his Gospel, Mark leaves us with the mystery of what really did happen to Jesus, and this takes us straight back into the heart of the story, to read once again about Jesus, who transformed the lives of everyone he met. The conclusion that the reader is compelled to draw is that this Gospel is about life, not about death, and about a life that has no end, because the life of Jesus continues to transform people's lives. The resurrection, rather than being tied to the time and place of the story, is left as an open book to the reader, who, rather than commemorating or disputing a moment in history, is given the chance to discover the reality of resurrection in their own experience.

The Gospel that has no ending, then, is not a literary failure but a profound statement. What happened on that strange morning? Where was Jesus if he wasn't in the tomb? Where is he now? Is he really alive or was it all a fairytale? You, the reader, must decide.

[1 January]

Waiting and longing

And behold, there was a man in Jerusalem, whose name was Simeon; and the same man was just and devout, waiting for the consolation of Israel; and the Holy Ghost was upon him. And it was revealed unto him by the Holy Ghost, that he should not see death, before he had seen the Lord's Christ. And he came by the Spirit into the temple; and when the parents brought in the child Jesus, to do for him after the custom of the law, then took he him up in his arms, and blessed God and said, 'Lord, now lettest thou thy servant depart in peace, according to thy word; for mine eyes have seen thy salvation, which thou hast prepared before the face of all people; a light to lighten the Gentiles, and the glory of thy people Israel.'

LUKE 2:25–32 (KJV)

Waiting is a recurring theme in the liturgical year. There is a nine-day period of waiting between Ascension Day and Pentecost. At his ascension (Luke 24:49) Jesus told his disciples to wait in Jerusalem—not exactly how long to wait, or what for—just to wait. And wait they did, until they were sure it was time to stop waiting. Lent is another season of waiting, although not so much waiting for something as waiting on—putting the rest of life on hold to wait in a consciously devoted way for the presence of God to pervade the soul. Lenten waiting has a wilderness quality to it—it involves a deprivation of the things of ordinary life in order to become one with God.

Waiting also features in Advent, but in this case, I think, there is a slightly different sense about it. This is a waiting with hope and anticipation for God to break into our world, a waiting suspended between beginnings and endings, in which every promise fulfilled becomes the beginning of yet another waiting. According to Christian tradition, the first Advent waiting was for the Messiah or Saviour to enter the world—an anticipation reflected in the promises of God to the patriarchs, the dreams of the prophets, and the prayers of generations of saints. The second Advent waiting is for the return of Christ in glory, heralding the end of this era. So Advent is about waiting for Christmas, but it's also waiting for the great 'Maranatha'—the cry of longing for the second coming of Christ into the world (see Revelation 22:20).

Waiting for the Messiah was not a passive waiting, but an aching, a longing, a reaching towards. Simeon, one of my favourite characters in the Gospels, had been on the alert, waiting for the Messiah, for a very long time indeed. He was waiting for the Messiah because he knew that he would not die until he'd seen him. But in a way, that knowledge adds a poignancy to the story. He wanted to see the Messiah—it seems that his life was focused around this waiting—yet he knew that once he had seen him, his own life would be over. Simeon waited, not passively but with an active seeking. I wonder how many young men, how many children, how many babies he had seen pass through the temple before his eyes alighted on Jesus. How many times had he asked, 'Is this the one, Lord?'

Through Advent, the practicalities of life usually mean that we are, quite literally, waiting for Christmas. There is something about following the themes of the Church year that draws us into that sense of waiting on God, waiting for his promise to be fulfilled. Yet the odd thing is that now that Advent is over, and Christmas is over, and New Year is upon us, the sense of waiting and longing doesn't go away. It may be that Christmas was a bit of a let-down. Unfortunately, the grand commercial build-up to the festival sometimes raises expectations so high that people end up feeling more washed out than fulfilled and blessed. Yet even if you had a wonderful Christmas, with dreams come true, it is still possible to arrive at the New Year with a sense that the horizon has once again fallen away; you may have a hunch that, once again, there is more life to live, more to do, more to find. We don't always know quite what it is we're waiting for. It seems to be part of the human condition that we get bored when we are too satisfied and, whenever one chapter of achievements or life events closes, we cannot rest too long before we sense that familiar feeling of reaching out for something more.

There is a paradox in this that sums up so much of our faith: the drive to reach out, move forward and make something happen is constrained by the need to wait on, wait for, the initiative of God's Spirit. We cannot force the work of God, but neither can we go to sleep on the job. I suppose that gives us our model of waiting for Christ's coming in glory, too, although here—perhaps like waiting for Pentecost, or for death—the promise has little tangible shape to it because it is a matter of waiting for something beyond our experience. We have no categories or pictures with which to describe what it means to say that Christ will come again in glory. We just know, somehow, that while we live in celebration that God has broken into our world, yet we are still waiting and longing for something more. This is not a passive waiting, though, not a case of lying back despondently, waiting for God to come and fix things. It's living while we wait, building the kingdom of heaven in the only life that we know we have, and feeding it from a deep well of hopeful dissatisfaction. Waiting and longing.

I love the words of Simeon—a very, very old man who had spent his whole life longing for the salvation of Israel. Did he know what he was waiting for? Probably not, in exact terms. But somehow, when he saw Jesus, he just knew that this child, at last, was what it was all about. Simeon's proclamation was what all those years of prayer and watchfulness had been for, all that attentiveness and discipline and sheer commitment on days that seemed unremarkable. 'Now, Lord,' he said, 'I can die happy. Now I've seen the thing I've been waiting for all my life. I've done what I came here for. I am fulfilled. *Nunc dimittis*: now you can let me go.'

John Coltrane, the jazz saxophonist, is famous all over the world for his beautiful music. The interesting thing about jazz is that, more than any other kind of music, every performance is unique. One night, Coltrane performed 'A Love Supreme', one of his most famous pieces, and as he played, every last ounce of his skill and musicianship seemed to come together in an absolutely magical performance. Just that one time, he was even better than the best. Everything about that performance was sublime, and when he'd finished, as he walked offstage, his drummer heard him breathe two words: '*Nunc dimittis*'. It was a unique moment of glory and Coltrane himself recognized that there was something beyond human accolades going on. Somehow he had touched heaven and he knew that he had done what he came for. The glory of God is revealed in those magic moments when we are touched by something beyond human achievement, when we see the presence of God break into the ordinary and there is a sense that life has been fulfilled. Heaven and earth collide.

[2 January]

Shepherds and wise men

My soul clings to the dust;
revive me according to your word.
When I told of my ways, you answered me;
teach me your statutes.
Make me understand the way of your precepts,
and I will meditate on your wondrous works.
My soul melts away for sorrow;
strengthen me according to your word.
Put false ways far from me;
and graciously teach me your law.
I have chosen the way of faithfulness;
I set your ordinances before me.
I cling to your decrees, O Lord;
let me not be put to shame.
I run the way of your commandments,
for you enlarge my understanding.

PSALM 119:25–32

In the time of King Herod, after Jesus was born in Bethlehem of Judea, wise men from the East came to Jerusalem, asking, 'Where is the child who has been born king of the Jews? For we observed his star at its rising, and have come to pay him homage.'

MATTHEW 2:1–2

The kings, or wise men, or magi, are traditionally celebrated at Epiphany, on 6 January. The way that we tend to conflate the Gospel accounts, plus the effect of our nativity plays and scenes, gives the impression that the wise men arrived at the stable about ten minutes after the shepherds, making a nice tableau. Reading between the lines, though, it's more likely that the men from the east arrived many months later.

It is perhaps more interesting to reflect on the different ways in which the shepherds and the magi found their way to Jesus. The shepherds came on the very night that Jesus was born, directed by an angelic revelation. They came to know about the newborn king suddenly and without warning, and their response was immediate and heartfelt. But the wise men had been studying the stars and planets for a long time, had travelled from far afield, and arrived in Bethlehem some time after the baby was born. The shepherds found their way to Jesus by revelation, and found themselves worshipping almost before they knew what had happened, but the wise men found their way there through study, work and long years of education. What's the best way to find our way to Jesus? By work or by revelation?

I don't know that the Church actually disapproves of intellectual effort, but it seems to me there is something of a tendency to favour revelation over formal theology. Somehow the idea prevails that faith that is acquired intellectually and carefully thought out over time is somehow inferior to, or not quite as real as, faith that depends on experience, emotion and instinct, appealing to the heart rather than the head.

Yet these things go rather in trends, and the truth is that the pursuit of faith has always required a combination of thought and feeling, work and inspiration. The psalmist prays in today's passage for inspiration—which, as he writes, does not seem to be forthcoming—but his method of seeking God was a devotion to study, careful thought and learning.

It's not uncommon to hear about people being discouraged from studying theology 'in case it ruins their faith'. Some years ago, I was on the brink of leaving London for Cambridge, to study theology in the university and to begin to prepare for ordination. There was no shortage of people who warned me about the dangers of this plan and about how too much thinking can knock faith off-course.

What actually happened was that studying theology from an academic perspective came as a huge relief. I had all sorts of questions about the Bible, about doctrine and philosophy and about my own faith, and here was a place where there was not only permission to air those questions but even a requirement to do so. Whether I emerged with faith or no faith was not the concern of the university. Clear thinking and thorough scholarship were top of the agenda. I quickly found, however, that among the lecturers and professors were many people of faith (some Christians, and some of other faiths) and they were not afraid to hold their faith open to all kinds of questions. They were also willing to give their students space and time to ask the questions that connected up their academic studies and personal faith.

In the end, I found that being allowed to believe in a God who could stand up to any amount of questioning, however hard, made God seem more believable to me, not less. As the course began, I was delighted to find that it was not only allowable to think very hard and ask any and every question, but that letting the awkward and unanswerable questions out into the open began to strengthen rather than weaken my faith. Why? Because repressing awkward questions doesn't make them go away, but it does turn them into demons, creating the anxiety that if the questions are allowed out, as though from a Pandora's box, order will never be restored.

Studying theology for six years in Cambridge meant getting closely acquainted with the university library. Academic libraries seem to impose an unhurried approach to work. You often have to order the books you need and wait anything from an hour to a few days for them to arrive. So you may begin with a plan of work in mind, but the library imposes its own pace and eventually forces you into a mode of calm, quiet, unhurried discovery. Waiting for the book you thought you needed, you often follow an unplanned lead. Some of my most interesting avenues of research occurred by reading the book that was filed next to the book I was really waiting for.

Some years later, I was going through a particularly barren patch in my life when I was struggling with a bereavement. I remember talking to another priest about my frustration with church and worship. 'I simply can't find God in the chapel,' I remember saying to her. 'Everyone else seems to be connected to God, and I just feel the whole thing is a mockery.' This wise woman, instead of trying to persuade me that God really was in the chapel, asked me, 'Well, where do you find the presence of God? Where, in all your daily life, is there a moment of deep peace where you feel that life and hope are possible?' I thought for a while. Deep peace? Life and hope? There was one place where I always found that. 'The library,' I said.

Isn't it true, in the end, that there is more than one way to find our way to Jesus? It may be by study, enquiry and a steady route through reading and debate, or it may be an experience that grabs us by the heart and won't let us go. I think it's probably true that most of us need a mixture of both, but it doesn't matter which route we take and which gifts we bring. The issue is not how we get there but whether, in the end, we arrive with fellow travellers in the presence of Jesus.

[3 January]

Double-edged prophecy

When the time came for their purification according to the law of Moses, they brought [Jesus] up to Jerusalem to present him to the Lord (as it is written in the law of the Lord, 'Every firstborn male shall be designated as holy to the Lord'), and they offered a sacrifice according to what is stated in the law of the Lord, 'a pair of turtle-doves or two young pigeons'…

Then Simeon blessed them and said to his mother Mary, 'This child is destined for the falling and the rising of many in Israel, and to be a sign that will be opposed so that the inner thoughts of many will be revealed—and a sword will pierce your own soul too.' There was also a prophet, Anna the daughter of Phanuel, of the tribe of Asher. She was of a great age, having lived with her husband for seven years after her marriage, then as a widow to the age of eighty-four. She never left the temple but worshipped there with fasting and prayer night and day. At that moment she came, and began to praise God and to speak about the child to all who were looking for the redemption of Jerusalem.

LUKE 2:22–24, 34–38

The presentation of a newly born child was a traditional rite of thanksgiving and dedication, not dissimilar to the baptism or dedication services that we are familiar with in church. There was nothing remarkable about Jesus being presented; he would have been one among many children dedicated to God in this way. But what was remarkable was that two temple prophets picked him out among the crowds and identified him as special and different. Over and over again in the birth narratives we see this pattern of an unremarkable event being suddenly transformed into something remarkable.

As each of these episodes has unfolded, they have gradually taken more and more of the world and brought it into contact with God through the incarnate Christ. All ages, types and classes of people are represented in these stories, so that God's act of redemption is acknowledged within every part of life and for all kinds of people, communities and relationships. The first to hear the angels' proclamations were Jesus' own family, placing the incarnation within the most intimate relationships and the ordinariness of everyday life. Then the angels called the shepherds, people who worked right on the edges of society, and brought them to worship. The magi found their way to Bethlehem by studying the stars, and so the story includes the wise, the rich, the privileged and the educated; the magi also represent the universality and inclusiveness of redemption, which extends far beyond the limits of culture or religious tradition. Finally, at the presentation of the baby in the temple, a perfectly ordinary religious rite is marked out as extraordinary, completing the picture by placing the recognition of Christ within the context of religious tradition.

The prophet Anna perceived the fulfilment of the messianic hope within this otherwise commonplace religious rite. Her immediate response was to give thanks to God, but then she began to spread the news to those who, like her, had been watching and waiting through difficult years for the fulfilment of God's promise. We are told that she spoke about the child 'to all who were looking for the redemption of Jerusalem' (v. 38). The Greek word for 'redemption' here is *lutrosis*, which can mean ransom, deliverance and liberation. Anna identified the baby as the Messiah, and in doing so became one of the first to proclaim the gospel, the new covenant.

The prophetic recognition of Christ in this story, however, is not only a message of comfort in the sense of a kind of comfort-blanket. It has an element of exhortation and encouragement about it, and Simeon's words give the double edge to the message: a warning, simultaneously, of comfort and discomfort. He extended the messianic hope of ancient Israel to become a universal hope, a promise of salvation for the whole world, but after this public prophecy, he gave a far more sombre and personal message in his private words to Mary, Jesus' mother: 'This child is destined for the falling and the rising of many in Israel, and to be a sign that will be opposed so that the inner thoughts of many will be revealed—and a sword will pierce your own soul too' (vv. 34–35).

Back in the stable, we saw Mary pondering while others rejoiced. Now, as Anna spreads a buzz of anticipation through the temple that the long-awaited Messiah has come, Simeon gives Mary more to ponder in this personal message—like a price tag to be picked up by those who come close to Jesus. Redemption comes at a price, paid not only by Jesus himself but also by those who encounter him at close quarters, whether in deep personal love or in antagonism and conflict. The prophet Malachi anticipated the heaviness of this price in his words, 'Who can endure the day of his coming, and who can stand when he appears?' (Malachi 3:2). Those who encountered Christ would not be unchanged: some would rise, and some would fall. Those who opposed the love and the order of God would find their lives in chaotic conflict, but even those who loved him would not necessarily remain unscathed. Even Mary would find her own soul riven in two.

It would be nice to believe that redemption is painless—that God might somehow swoop in from on high and solve our problems, stop our wars, resolve our conflicts and heal our diseases. But Simeon's double-edged prophecy highlights the fact that there is nothing comfortable about the Christian message of salvation. The Christian gospel is not magic, wishing away all ills. It is given in incarnation, the inseparable fusing together of the human and divine, and grows at the same pace as all human life—slowly. The unwritten years of Christ's life on earth between the presentation and the beginning of his ministry were the years in which he grew in grace and wisdom, learning how to live out his destiny as the incarnate Son of God. The Christian account of redemption was not delivered swiftly from on high, but emerged slowly and carefully in the lives of real human beings.

Redemption, then, does not wipe away human flaws and failings or iron out our quirks and idiosyncrasies. Instead it has a transforming effect, so that even in our imperfection we can give glory to God. Also, because redemption is effected through incarnation, it implies relationship with God and with other people—and although this is initiated by God and enabled through his grace, it is fulfilled only in our response. Salvation is not worked on us over our heads. It is realized as we cooperate with God, allowing our lives to be transformed, sometimes through painful struggle, into his likeness. What's more, it is made real not only individually but in community. We are partakers in one another's redemption, and we can ease or antagonize one another's experience as we are transformed into Jesus' likeness.

The story of the presentation at the temple celebrates our redemption and commemorates the reception and acknowledgment of Christ into the formal structures of religious rite. And it stands as an invitation not merely to commemorate a historic event, but to welcome God's promised redemption into our lives, despite its implied discomfort, cooperating with his transforming work in our lives and in the lives of those around us.

[4 January]

Born in a borrowed room

And she gave birth to her firstborn son and wrapped him in bands of cloth, and laid him in a manger, because there was no place for them in the inn.

LUKE 2:7

Then came the day of Unleavened Bread, on which the Passover lamb had to be sacrificed. So Jesus sent Peter and John, saying, 'Go and prepare the Passover meal for us that we may eat it.' They asked him, 'Where do you want us to make preparations for it?' 'Listen,' he said to them, 'when you have entered the city, a man carrying a jar of water will meet you; follow him into the house he enters and say to the owner of the house, "The teacher asks you, 'Where is the guest room, where I may eat the Passover with my disciples?'" He will show you a large room upstairs, already furnished. Make preparations for us there.' So they went and found everything as he had told them; and they prepared the Passover meal.

LUKE 22:7–13

These two moments from Luke's Gospel give us a connection between the beginning and the end of the life of Jesus. We've already considered various ways in which beginnings and endings are important in interpretation. Sometimes the way significant points in a book are connected up also serves to highlight important features about the story. Here we have two moments—not the opening or closing chapters of Luke's Gospel, but at the opening and closing moments of Jesus' life.

Luke, of all the Gospel writers, is the master of the technique of 'wrapping' one story between two little related paragraphs, which in themselves give an interpretative clue to the whole. An example of this technique is the two stories in Luke 8:40–56, in which the story of the woman who has been bleeding for twelve years is inserted inside the story of the twelve-year-old girl who has died. The chronic nature of the woman's pain is highlighted by the fact that she has been ill for the whole of the girl's life. There is something remarkable about the fact that Jesus stops for the woman, whose illness made her socially unacceptable, and that he is touched by her, which would have made him ritually unclean too. But the story is made all the more powerful by the fact that Jesus meets the woman on the way towards the house of a synagogue leader—a person for whom ritual cleanliness would have been highly important. The way Luke wraps one story around the other increases the impact of each. A similar kind of effect is created here by the fact that Jesus starts and ends his life in borrowed rooms.

We read on 25 December that Jesus was born far from home, in very ordinary surroundings, in the room where the animals were kept, because there was no room in the inn (*kataluma*). We don't know exactly whether that was due to pressure of space and an act of kindness, or because of a grudging rejection by the relatives of the holy family. But either way, Jesus was born in a borrowed room.

Thirty-something years later, as his life neared an end, his life began to wind down in another borrowed room—another *kataluma*, for the 'guest room' that Jesus sent his disciples to find is the same word in Greek as was used for 'inn' in Luke 2:7.

As the end of his life neared, he must have known that his enemies were closing in: he could read the signs. But it is always the case with prophets and social revolutionaries that the moment comes when they have to choose—either to quieten down and disappear in order to survive, or to continue on their all-consuming mission and risk the consequences. Joan of Arc did it; Dietrich Bonhoeffer did it; Martin Luther King did it. In each case, their mission was life-consuming; and in each case, in the end, they paid for it with their lives.

Jesus must have known he was living on the edge that week in

Jerusalem. He probably knew that he was unlikely to make it through the weekend in one piece unless he 'disappeared'. He'd escaped capture before. His first sermon in Nazareth enraged the congregation so much that they carried him up to a cliff top in order to throw him off—a popular alternative to stoning someone to death for blasphemy. But Jesus, mysteriously, slipped through the crowds that time, and perhaps on other occasions too (Luke 4:30).

This time was different, though. Was it the intensity of his mission, or the build-up of his message, or the size of his following, or the fact that he was finally in Jerusalem and there was nowhere to go from there except into obscurity? We'll never know for sure, but something told Jesus that the time was now. This time he couldn't just slip through the crowds or move to another town and carry on. This time the consequences of his mission were inescapable: he must either see it through to a dangerous end or give the whole thing up. And this time he decided not to disappear. Instead, on his last night of freedom, he borrowed a guest room and celebrated the Passover feast with his friends.

The room he borrowed was a place he had borrowed before. He knew where it was, and he was known to the proprietor. I wonder whether Jesus thought of the connection between the borrowed rooms where his life began and ended. Maybe it was so commonplace for him, as an itinerant who travelled light, that it seemed like just one more room. There was a time in my life when I travelled a great deal, singing and playing, and travelling by air or road. I slept on planes and in sleeper compartments, and stayed in all sorts of places. I remember many of my hosts, but I hardly remember any of the rooms. After a while they all look the same.

There's a vulnerability to borrowed space. The Englishman's home may be his castle, but it doesn't have quite the same sense of privacy and security if it's a rented castle. You can never quite pull up the drawbridge in borrowed space. That was part of Jesus' vulnerability for us: he didn't lord it over us but slummed it along with the ordinary people, starting and ending his life in borrowed rooms.

There is also, though, a tremendous freedom of spirit that comes with travelling light, perhaps echoing the nomadic spirit (see 9 December). You certainly live in a place while you are there, and make it your home. You occupy it fully and take responsibility for cleaning up before you leave. But there is something significant about not owning the space you occupy. I particularly like the Australian Aboriginal idea that we belong to the land rather than the land belonging to us. All those years on the road have left me with a lifetime habit of decluttering. Too much 'stuff' makes me feel a bit trapped and weighed down.

Jesus, then, after three years of itinerant preaching and ministry, went in search of a *kataluma* in which to celebrate the Passover with his friends. Then, what was predicted in the temple (Luke 2:34–35) began to be fulfilled as everything started to unravel at the Last Supper. Even though the sting of rejection was still there, because it was one of his own friends who betrayed him, this time there was room in the inn, and this time he was welcome. As T.S. Eliot put it so eloquently, 'And the end of all our exploring / Will be to arrive where we started / And know the place for the first time.'[6]

[5 January]

Kings and gifts

In the time of King Herod, after Jesus was born in Bethlehem of Judea, wise men from the East came to Jerusalem, asking, 'Where is the child who has been born king of the Jews? For we observed his star at its rising, and have come to pay him homage.' When King Herod heard this, he was frightened, and all Jerusalem with him; and calling together all the chief priests and scribes of the people, he inquired of them where the Messiah was to be born. They told him, 'In Bethlehem of Judea; for so it has been written by the prophet: "And you, Bethlehem, in the land of Judah, are by no means least among the rulers of Judah; for from you shall come a ruler who is to shepherd my people Israel."' Then Herod secretly called for the wise men and learned from them the exact time when the star had appeared. Then he sent them to Bethlehem, saying, 'Go and search diligently for the child; and when you have found him, bring me word so that I may also go and pay him homage.'

MATTHEW 2:1–8

The historical reality of the wise men from the east is pretty hard to establish. They were probably not kings at all. It was Tertullian, a second-century theologian, who linked them with the kings of the Psalms: 'May the kings of Tarshish and of the isles render him tribute, may the kings of Sheba and Seba bring gifts' (Psalm 72:10). Later, the Church used this text to describe the magi in the liturgy for Epiphany, and so the magi became 'kings' in the popular imagination. It's much more likely that they were experts in the science of astronomy, and possibly also Zoroastrian priests. Ancient astronomy was a very respectable occupation, tracking the movement of the stars in some kind of pre-scientific study of the heavens.

A few years back, a BBC programme offered a more risqué suggestion, however—that the wise men were in fact astrologers, whose horoscope charts predicted the birth of a new world ruler.

Horoscopes, of course, are vaguely associated with the dark arts and therefore generally out of favour among Christians, yet we are often quite ready to rule out one means of obtaining knowledge while accepting others without question. The commercialization of horoscopes, quite apart from any association with the dark arts, is a sound reason for dismissing them, but we can be too easily seduced into thinking that rationalist means of obtaining knowledge are 'safe' and therefore compatible with Christian thinking.

Even today in the East, intellectual and spiritual wisdom are not divorced from each other, as they tend to be in the West. Too much respect for Western intellectualism can be just as bad for spiritual wisdom as a dodgy horoscope. In order to begin to understand God, we have to learn an approach to knowledge that, while including rational thought, does not limit itself to empiricism or give in to the kind of intellectual arrogance which assumes that what we cannot see cannot be real.

Despite their wisdom and the accuracy of their journey, however, once they arrived in the vicinity of Bethlemen the wise men almost fell at the last hurdle by making assumptions of their own. Because they were searching for a king, they went to King Herod's palace. In doing so, they set off a series of events that ended in the massacre of many small children (Matthew 2:16), and threatened the very miracle they had come to seek. The knowledge of God is often hidden in unexpected places. The wise men sought God in a palace and discovered him among a humble family. We might fruitlessly seek God in a church or in a library, only to find him unexpectedly in the company of a crumpled homeless figure in a doorway.

It's a tradition in most cultures to bring gifts to a newly born child. The gifts mean nothing to the baby, of course, who is only interested in being warm, fed and comfortable, but they celebrate new life, represent a welcome into the community, and are often chosen with the parents in mind. When my son was born, one of my favourite gifts was perhaps the least practical of all. My next-door neighbours came to the hospital with a tiny replica pair of those very trendy baseball boots—so small that by the time my son was big enough to wear shoes, he had already outgrown them. But they were humorous and, as a miniature version of the boots that I wore myself, they symbolized his welcome into the community.

Jesus was offered quite a lot of gifts when he was born. There was the simple gift of emergency hospitality—a quiet place in an animal's stall within a peasant household. There shepherds came and worshipped, offering nothing more than their praise. The wise men, however, came with gifts for the newborn king. It has often been said, either in humour or in cynicism, that their gifts were fairly useless for a new baby, with the possible exception of the gold. Symbolically, though, they proclaim Jesus to be both priest and king: gold is a gift for a king, while frankincense was (and still is) burnt in religious ceremonies. Myrrh, however, is an embalming product and prophesied his death.

Jesus is seen here receiving gifts and worship from people of other nationalities and religions. These men were not converts; rather they recognized something great in a context other than their own. The Church often waits for people to affirm their beliefs before we will accept the genuineness of their worship. Perhaps these visitors to the holy child act as a reminder that God does not stand at the door of the church, checking people's doctrinal credentials before he will receive their worship.

Because they came from far away, with unfamiliar philosophies and religious ideas, the magi are often taken to symbolize the inclusiveness of the gospel. The sweetness of nativity scenes, though, while not entirely inappropriate given that a new baby is centre stage, can hide the fact that a genuinely inclusive gospel is uncomfortable to live out. We let ourselves off the hook too easily if, privately or unconsciously, we think that once people encounter Christ they should fit in with our idea of what a Christian should be like. The reality is that even those who do acknowledge Christ will inevitably bring with them different interpretations of God and church, if they come from a cultural background other than our own. The challenge to us is to treat this as their gift, rather than a problem that needs to be ironed out.

An even more challenging idea, though, is to expand our concept of the inclusiveness of the gospel to acknowledge those who will treat Christ with respect and bring him gifts but not necessarily become signed-up Christians. This shouldn't really strike us as extraordinary. Many scholars argue that the long, slow history of ancient Israelite religion shows a developing idea of who God was. The oldest parts of the Old Testament speak of many gods—of whom the God of Israel was but one, and then, later, the greatest among many. It was an even later idea that there was only one God and that other gods were mere idols. It seems, also, that the refinement of the Israelites' theology was inspired by other religious systems. Borrowing ideas and learning from other religions is not necessarily going to damage our faith or make all religions identical. There is a difference between changing our idea of God and changing our idea of our own understanding. Being too static in belief is just as likely to lead us into error as being too uncritical in our thinking.

Some of the most interesting encounters I have had in recent years have been conversations between intellectuals of the three faiths 'of the book'—Christians, Muslims and Jews. It has been the greatest privilege to learn from people outside my own tradition, and a mutually enriching experience to discover that we really can tread with deep respect into each other's territory in order to learn from one another rather than to convert one another. The gifts of such visitors to the Church are valuable and should be made welcome.

Such ideas of welcome and inclusiveness, however, cannot hide the fact that Jesus did not promise to bring ease or comfort. True religion takes on difficult issues like poverty and injustice, and, because it does, conflict will inevitably follow. Behind the high altar in the chapel of King's College in Cambridge hangs Rubens' magnificent painting, *The Adoration of the Magi* (1634). It depicts three figures of different ages and different nationalities, bowing before the holy child and his mother. They offer their gifts, including a swinging thurible of incense. If you stand very close to the painting, you can detect in the brush strokes that the thurible had originally been painted about ten inches further to the left, and Rubens later altered the composition of the painting. What you can also see, however, is the evidence of an act of vandalism when, in the 1970s, the letters 'IRA' were slashed across the middle of the painting. After painstaking repair, all that remains is the scratch marks of those letters, still faintly visible in the surface of the paint. The painting, then, not only embodies the inclusiveness of the gospel to all nationalities and ages, but also bears the pain of political frustration and violence. Viewed simply as a work of art, the act of vandalism is incomprehensible. Viewed as a religious icon, though, the vandals' mark is a reminder that God is embodied not only in the sweetness of a newborn baby but also in the suffering Christ, whose face was 'marred... beyond human semblance' and who was 'wounded for our transgressions, crushed for our iniquities' (Isaiah 52:14; 53:5).

[6 January]

The end is a new beginning: returning by another way

Having been warned in a dream not to return to Herod, [the wise men] left for their own country by another road. Now after they had left, an angel of the Lord appeared to Joseph in a dream and said, 'Get up, take the child and his mother, and flee to Egypt, and remain there until I tell you; for Herod is about to search for the child, to destroy him.' Then Joseph got up, took the child and his mother by night, and went to Egypt, and remained there until the death of Herod. This was to fulfil what had been spoken by the Lord through the prophet, 'Out of Egypt I have called my son.' …

When Herod died, an angel of the Lord suddenly appeared in a dream to Joseph in Egypt and said, 'Get up, take the child and his mother, and go to the land of Israel, for those who were seeking the child's life are dead.' Then Joseph got up, took the child and his mother, and went to the land of Israel. But when he heard that Archelaus was ruling over Judea in place of his father Herod, he was afraid to go there. And after being warned in a dream, he went away to the district of Galilee. There he made his home in a town called Nazareth, so that what had been spoken through the prophets might be fulfilled, 'He will be called a Nazorean.'

MATTHEW 2:12–15, 19–23

I remember once travelling to the other side of the world, beginning at Gatwick on a pleasant, sunny September morning. There wasn't a cloud in the sky and the conditions were perfect for travel, but there was a problem with the plane. First we boarded late; then there was a false start, after which all the passengers were herded out on to the tarmac and on to another plane. The plane took off eventually, several hours late, and by the time we reached the first stopover the whole journey had been completely disrupted. What began as a 21-hour flight with one refuelling stop became a three-day journey with unexpected visits to exotic places.

My travelling partner was a far more experienced and jaded traveller than I, and she got out her Walkman and eyeshades and treated it as one more annoying delay to her schedule. But I had never travelled right round the world before, and to me it didn't seem like just another bus ride. I decided that if I was making unscheduled stops in three places I'd never visited before, I might as well take in the experience—and what an experience it turned out to be! I had expected only to have time for a quick breakfast and a coffee in Houston before boarding another plane. Instead, the journey took me to Los Angeles, where I saw a film studio and was later woken in the early hours of the morning by an earth tremor—not exactly a pleasant experience but a fascinating one. The next night, I spent four hours late in the evening in a beautiful Buddhist garden in Hawaii, full of the rich, heady smell of jasmine and hibiscus flowers. It was my first experience of a climate where it remains intensely warm after dark, and that evening in the garden stands out in my memory as one of my life's best moments. The next day I had a close-up view of the volcanic landscape of New Zealand as we touched down to refuel in Auckland before finally arriving at my destination in Australia. Had I put on the earphones and eyeshades like my neighbour, I would have missed all this. Instead, I let these strange diversions become a rich memory that has stayed with me for years afterwards.

The end of the nativity story comes with an account of two sets of travel plans being completely and stressfully disrupted. We read of the exit first of the magi, and then of the holy family, from Bethlehem. These rushed and anxious journeys create a sense of conclusion to the nativity story, even though there is nothing conclusive about the individual stories of the magi and the holy family. If this were a fairytale, there would be some kind of happy-ever-after conclusion. Instead, the characters scatter from the stage in opposite directions and, as the curtain goes down on this particular scene, we are left wondering what happened next.

Apart from the little vignette that Luke provides about Jesus as a twelve-year-old boy (2:41–52), the story tails off abruptly here and doesn't resume until Jesus is about 30. Like the best literature, not all the ends of the story are neatly tied up! So we know very little about what happened next, either to the magi or to the holy family. The magi have played their part in the story, their lives continue and we never hear any more about them. Beyond the journeys to Egypt and then north to Nazareth, we have little detail, either, about what happened to the family until Jesus reaches adulthood.

Nevertheless, as Matthew tells the story, it's not a neatly wrapped-up ending, but a scene of urgent and slightly panicky journey-making. Both the magi and the holy family are warned not to go back the way they came, and they depart from Bethlehem in different directions. In each case, their plans are disrupted and they have to reschedule at short notice. They undoubtedly had to improvise to a certain extent. As anyone knows who has ever been caught up in a delayed flight or an airport security crisis, last-minute changes to travel plans defy the confidence and comfort of careful planning. Flexibility and improvisation are called for—or forced upon travellers. The end of the nativity story, then, marks the beginning of two new journeys into the unknown—two journeys in which the plans are changed at the last minute and departure is suddenly made urgent.

The idea that we cannot go back the way we have come is an important spiritual metaphor: having encountered the Christ-child, we can never just go back. Even if we return to the same life, we find that it has somehow changed. This is by no means a new idea. Pope Leo the Great wrote that the change of plan in the magis' journey home was not only to baffle Herod's murderous plan, but also that 'it behoved them now that they believed in Christ not to walk in the paths of their old line of life, but having entered on a new way to keep away from the errors they had left'.[7]

We never find out anything more about the magi; we simply know that, having encountered Jesus, they cannot return the same way. He continued to affect their lives after the moment of acknowledgment and worship; their lives changed direction because of this encounter. Similarly with Jesus' family: they found that this child, small and vulnerable though he was, and so early in his life, compelled them to make urgent and unplanned journeys to ensure their safety.

This story gives us an image of God's interaction with us during times of change—both in the idea that there is always the possibility of new avenues opening up for us, and also that when change comes at us like an alarm bell, unsought and unwelcome, God provides guidance through the stress of 'fight or flight'. It is often the case that clarity in decision-making can come to us in the midst of an emergency: without any time to consider the options, we see the right course of action and we are led through the storm.

Stress and change, then, can come to us either as a welcome opening of new horizons or as a necessity to act in an urgent situation for which we feel unprepared. To have these ideas presented to us as the ending of the nativity story leaves it very far from a neat closure. Rather, we see Jesus' family and the wise men being pushed out into new and unfamiliar surroundings, changed for ever by their encounter with this holy child. The nativity story does not have a neatly tied-up ending, but a rather dramatic exit into the unknown, the only certainty being that there will never be a return to business as usual. For those who like the idea that the gospel gives us certainty—clear and applicable truths that we can solidly depend upon—this ending to the birth narratives is an uncomfortable disruption. The only certainty here is the promise of uncertainty. But it is an uncertainty that is full of hope, for it is also the promise of new beginnings.

NOTES

1 C. Leonard Woolley, *Ur Excavations, Vol.II: The Royal Cemetery*, British Museums Publications and University of Pennsylvania Museum, 1934
2 *Christian Century*, Nov 14 2006
3 *Common Worship: Services and Prayers for the Church of England*, Church House Publishing
4 Elizabeth Goudge, *The Joy of Snow*, Hodder & Stoughton, 1974
5 John Fowles, *The French Lieutenant's Woman*, Jonathan Cape, 1969
6 T.S. Eliot, 'Little Gidding' V, *Four Quartets*, Faber & Faber
7 Leo the Great, Sermon XXXIII, 'On the Feast of the Epiphany', III, iv

Journey to Jerusalem

Bible readings from Ash Wednesday to Easter Sunday

David Winter

'Twelve young men were walking with their leader along a road about 30 miles north of Galilee, in a hilly area where the river Jordan had its source. As they walked, their leader put two questions to them, and the answer to the second one would have profound consequences not just for them but eventually for the whole world. The leader was Jesus. The twelve young men (and they were young, most of them barely in their 20s) were his disciples.'

This book follows the journey of Jesus and his followers to Jerusalem—the story of the culmination of his ministry in the events of Good Friday and Easter, the story of the 'good news of God' for the whole world. It is this story that shapes the faith and life of every Christian. As we reflect on these events, like the disciples we can experience the awakening of faith in Jesus and hear the challenge to follow him, wherever he leads. With them we can tread the path to Gethsemane and Golgotha, and on to the empty tomb and new life.

ISBN 978 1 84101 485 2 £7.99
Available from your local Christian bookshop or, in case of difficulty, direct from BRF using the order form on page 175.

The Rite Stuff

Ritual in contemporary Christian worship and mission

Ed. Pete Ward

Ritual is having something of a revival in church, as some Christians start to explore ways of prayer and worship from more ancient traditions. In the past, ritual has sometimes been derided as 'empty', but in fact it focuses meaning. It can help us express our feelings for fellow believers and at the same time lift us into the presence of our God.

This book is a follow-up to *Mass Culture* (BRF 1999), which looked at the Communion service and its continued significance for worship and mission in today's culture. In *The Rite Stuff*, each chapter explores a different aspect of ritual and faith. The range of these discussions is quite wide, but the unifying factor is the growing appreciation of the significance of ritual for worship and spirituality in postmodernity.

The seven chapters are written by Jonny Baker, Maggi Dawn, Ana Draper, Jeremy Fletcher, Anthony Reddie, Mike Riddell and Pete Ward.

ISBN 978 1 84101 227 8   £8.99
Available from your local Christian bookshop or, in case of difficulty, direct from BRF using the order form on page 175.

The Promise of Christmas

Reflections for the Advent season

Fleur Dorrell

'During this Advent season, we celebrate God's incarnation, we hold on to our hope in his future kingdom and know that one day we really will meet him in glory.'

This book of readings offers a way of preparing ourselves for the celebration of Christmas by reflecting on the promises and prophecies found throughout the Bible, which look forward to Christ's coming. Going back to the very beginning of creation, we see how God reaches out to his people, longing to draw them closer, no matter how often they turn from him. As we approach the festival of Emmanuel—God with us—we can let his love warm our hearts as, despite life's busyness, we choose to linger in his presence.

ISBN 978 1 84101 214 8   £4.99
Available from your local Christian bookshop or, in case of difficulty, direct from BRF using the order form on page 175.

When the Time Was Right

Bible readings for the Advent season

Stephen Rand

Christmas was no accident. The Bible tells us that Jesus was born at just the right time: God's plans and purposes worked out over centuries, bearing fruit in a moment that changed the history of the world. In this book of readings for Advent, we meet the kind of people God uses: the failures, the reluctant, the ordinary, the humble, the faithful and the persevering. In fact, they are people like us, and we all have a part to play in God's ongoing purposes.

The first Christmas was an enormously significant moment in what is still an unfolding picture. The Christmas and Easter purposes of God will be fulfilled in the second Advent: the ultimate overthrow of evil and the release of the entire universe from the effects of sin. Best of all, those who put their faith and trust in the one who was born, died and rose again become members of the royal family of heaven and share in the triumph of the victor. This Christmas you can go back in time—and anticipate the future!

ISBN 978 1 84101 486 9 £7.99
Available from your local Christian bookshop or, in case of difficulty, direct from BRF using the order form on page 175.

ADVENT AND LENT BOOKS FROM BRF

Did you know BRF publishes a new Lent and Advent book each year? All our Lent and Advent books are designed with a daily printed Bible reading, comment and reflection. Some can be used in groups and contain questions which can be used in a study or reading group.

If you would like to be kept in touch with information about our forthcoming Lent or Advent books, please complete the coupon below.

- ☐ Please keep me in touch by post with forthcoming Lent or Advent books
- ☐ Please email me with details about forthcoming Lent or Advent books

Email address: ____________________

Name ____________________

Address ____________________

____

____

Postcode ____________________

Telephone ____________________

Signature ____________________

Please send this completed form to:

BRF, FREEPOST,
First Floor, Elsfield Hall,
15–17 Elsfield Way,
OXFORD OX2 8FG

Tel. 01865 319700
Fax. 01865 319701
Email: enquiries@brf.org.uk

www.brf.org.uk

PROMO REF: END/ADVENT07

BRF is a Registered Charity

ORDER FORM

REF	TITLE	PRICE	QTY	TOTAL
485 2	*Journey to Jerusalem*	£7.99		
227 8	*The Rite Stuff*	£8.99		
214 8	*The Promise of Christmas*	£4.99		
486 9	*When the Time Was Right*	£7.99		
		Postage and packing:		
		Donation:		
		Total enclosed:		

POSTAGE AND PACKING CHARGES				
Order value	UK	Europe	Surface	Air Mail
£7.00 & under	£1.25	£3.00	£3.50	£5.50
£7.01–£30.00	£2.25	£5.50	£6.50	£10.00
Over £30.00	free	prices on request		

Name ______________________ Account Number ______________

Address ____

____ Postcode __________

Telephone Number ______________ Email ______________________

Payment by: ❑ Cheque ❑ Mastercard ❑ Visa ❑ Postal Order ❑ Maestro

Card no. ☐☐☐☐ ☐☐☐☐ ☐☐☐☐ ☐☐☐☐

Expires ☐☐ ☐☐ Security code ☐☐☐ Issue no. ☐☐☐

Signature ________________________________ Date __________

All orders must be accompanied by the appropriate payment.

Please send your completed order form to:
BRF, First Floor, Elsfield Hall, 15–17 Elsfield Way, Oxford OX2 8FG
Tel. 01865 319700 / Fax. 01865 319701 Email: enquiries@brf.org.uk

❑ Please send me further information about BRF publications.

Available from your local Christian bookshop. **BRF is a Registered Charity**

Resourcing your spiritual journey

through...

- Bible reading notes
- Books for Advent & Lent
- Books for Bible study and prayer
- Books to resource those working with under 11s in school, church and at home
- Quiet days and retreats
- Training for primary teachers and children's leaders
- Godly Play
- Barnabas RE Days

For more information, visit the **brf** website at **www.brf.org.uk**

BRF is a Registered Charity